ALL OUR YESTERDAYS

A Brief History of the National Guild for Community Arts Education 1967–2001

ALL OUR YESTERDAYS

A Brief History of the National Guild for Community Arts Education 1967–2001

By

Lolita Mayadas

www.bookstandpublishing.com

Published by
Bookstand Publishing
Pasadena, CA 91101
4826_6

ISBN 978-1-953710-00-0

In recognition of the passion and commitment of those who strive daily to make the arts accessible to all.

Contents

List of Photos

1991

1992

1994

1995

1998

2001

Undated

Endorsements

This impressive history of the National Guild for Community Arts Education by its long-time Executive Director, Lolita Mayadas, reflects her personal perspectives on the trials, tribulations, and rewards of growing a small, nearly defunct organization into a successful arts education association. Lolita beautifully engages the reader in the highs and lows of that journey, relaying a clear understanding of the passion, expertise, finesse and years of commitment necessary to nurture an arts organization and bring it into the national spotlight. It is rare to find as well-crafted, personalized, and well-executed an organizational history that is both a "good read," and a "must read" for arts leaders.

Scott Shanklin-Peterson,
Former Senior Deputy Chairman, National Endowment for the Arts.
Senior Fellow and former Director, College of Charleston Arts Management Program; SC.

In All Our Yesterdays, *Lolita Mayadas tells the story of a dozen settlement house music schools which grow to become the National Guild for Community Arts Education, worthy of a $3 million "Creative Communities" grant from HUD with additional support from the NEA. Prospective readers will be pleased to know that the charm, salience and precision of expression that distinguished Lolita as Guild Executive Director are reflected in her narrative style. Filled with entertaining anecdotes illustrating how creative, energetic, public-spirited, idiosyncratic individuals with strong artistic opinions really interact and make decisions, this book can serve as a primer for anyone contemplating association management or service.*

Jonathan Katz, Ph.D.
Professor of Practice in Cultural Policy and Arts Management, George Mason University;
Former CEO, National Assembly of State Arts Agencies (NASAA).

This carefully crafted history of the National Guild provides an important and personal perspective that only Lolita Mayadas could offer. She has carefully researched and recorded the history prior to her arrival. She has identified her own enormous successes, but has not ignored the challenges, both personal and professional, encountered in her 20 years of leadership. Lolita's thoughtful and well-documented history provides an important and helpful reminder of the foundation on which all of today's successes rest.

Lowell Noteboom,
Former Trustee and Board Chair, MacPhail Center for Music, Minneapolis, MN;
Former Vice-Chair and Trustee, National Guild for Community Arts Education.

This book relates the long, fascinating, and sometimes convoluted history of the National Guild for Community Arts Education. It is a must read for anyone interested in learning about the ups and downs of building an organization. Thoughtfully written, crisp and concise, it doesn't sugar coat anything. The reader will share the joys, sorrows, loneliness, and camaraderie of the experience and will note the sheer depth of conviction it took to effectively lead an association through both adversity and prosperity into its rightful place in the broader arts and education movement in America. I am impressed that Lolita was able to compile so much information with a clear timeline and cast of characters and keep me enthralled in the story line.

Helen Tuntland Jackson,
Past Executive Director, Hochstein School of Music and Dance, Rochester, NY;
Former Trustee, National Guild for Community Arts Education.

Acknowledgements

I am deeply indebted to numerous people who have helped bring this book to fruition. First, I want to thank Kathy Schumacher for her diligent and detailed reviews of the manuscript multiple times as my editor and for counseling me about the structure and design of the book. My thanks also go to Helen Jackson for offering another pair of eagle eyes to proofread the manuscript and correct factual errors and for writing an endorsement. Likewise, warm thanks to Scott Shanklin-Peterson, Jonathan Katz, and Lowell Noteboom for providing referrals and endorsements.

My gratitude goes to Gayle Morgan, Duffie Adelson, and Jonathan Herman for their generous gifts to support the publication and marketing of this book and to the National Guild for promoting it and providing additional support services.

I also wish to express my great appreciation to Dick Casper for writing the Foreword. Dick's perspectives are important since he (like Helen) was closely aligned with the Guild as a school director and later, as trustee through the entire period covered by this history. My gratitude also goes to all those who so generously gave me their time for extended interviews which helped to enhance the narrative and made it so much more fun to write: Dorothy Amarandos, Henry Bridges, Dick Casper, Richard W. Colburn, Marcy Horwitz, Dick Kauffman, Hadassah Markson, Halsey North, and Kal Novak. I also extend my thanks to Duffie Adelson, Eric Bachrach, Rachel Bellow, Jessica Chao, Ben Dunham, Richard Evans, David Lapin, Gayle Morgan, Kirsten Morgan, Peggy Quackenbush, and Mohan Subramaniam for feedback and advice, and to Jonathan Herman, Adam Johnston, and Claire Wilmoth at the National Guild for their help and support. Special thanks also to Jay Everett for his comments and for extensive work with the photographs.

And last, but by no means least, my deepest thanks go to Azim Mayadas for his unfailing encouragement, insightful critiques, and final proofreading. I also offer my great appreciation to our Three Graces: Ayesha, Tanya, and Priya for their enthusiastic support at all times. If I have inadvertently omitted anyone, I offer my apologies.

This project represents a labor of love for everyone involved in it. I hope we have succeeded in making this narrative both informative and readable for those who wish to learn more about the Guild's early years and also the achievements and challenges in the period that followed – one of the most dynamic in its long history.

Foreword

In common with everyone I ever knew, or even heard of, the thought of running a community school of the arts never crossed my mind. Yet when the opportunity came to be director of the Cape Cod Conservatory I gladly accepted. After all, I reasoned, I love music, had been teaching and playing concerts for years, was interested in business, and was ready for a change. What more did it take?

Over the next four months I learned to my dismay how much more it took. And that's when I heard about the National Guild and went off to St. Louis for my first Guild conference. What I found was salvation! Every problem, every impossible predicament I faced was familiar to the old hands in the Guild and many others, and they were all eager to share their solutions, their successes and even their failures! Even more reassuring, they were a phone call away year round and always happy to help with any problems. Inevitably, we all soon became friends.

Annual Guild conferences became not just an opportunity to solve problems and learn what was new and different but also to have some very good times. Whenever my wife, Elizabeth and I drive past the Union Oyster House in Boston we smile and recall an endless joy-filled evening forty years ago with several of our director friends, one of many such evenings during my thirty-one Guild conferences.

That the Guild even existed then was proof of the soundness of the role it served. After the messianic leadership of Herbert Zipper the Guild experienced a leadership vacuum which left it on artificial life support for several years until help came from the unlikeliest and most distant place – India, by way of London, Miami and Rochester, New York. Lolita Mayadas, in the words of past Guild Trustee, Lowell Noteboom,[1] "was a warm and gracious encourager and at the same time an absolute force of nature with strong views and the determination and political skill to see that they were put into action. Much of what the Guild is today has its roots in Lolita's vision and determination during that period." [2] A key piece of that vision was the hiring of Jonathan Herman, our highly effective CEO these past fifteen years.

Those of you who know only the smoothly functioning, well-staffed Guild of today may find it impossible to appreciate the nerve and iron will required for the Guild of the 1980's to survive and then thrive. How fortunate we are that Lolita has now given us a very readable, warts and all, history of our extraordinary organization. I can assure you that this history is far more enjoyable to read about or write about than it was to live through – especially for Lolita.

With a greatly expanded membership and solid management, there is every good reason to feel confident that this organization, which does so much to support, preserve, and expand the arts to which we have all devoted a lifetime will enjoy a secure but always adventurous future.

Richard Casper
Barnstable, Massachusetts

Preface

This is a tribute to an organization I knew and loved for more than twenty years. Whether it was blind luck or destiny that brought me to the Guild as Executive Director in 1981, I still marvel at the extraordinary opportunity given to me. Everything I had done beforehand seemed to happen in an accidental, random sort of way – running a music school overseas, teaching and working one-on-one with music and dance students at a community music school, heading a fledgling dance company, and assisting in public relations and development for a mid-sized orchestra. But each experience seemed to prepare me in more ways for the Guild than if I had laid down specific strategies to achieve that goal. On the way, in a serendipitous fashion, I seem to have developed an aptitude for building from the ground up.

At the time, the Guild was facing a looming crisis, with a loss of key board and staff leaders and a severe lack of resources. Perhaps that challenge alone intrigued and energized me. Or perhaps I possess some adventurous, even reckless, character traits. Regardless, what truly attracted me was the Guild itself: its unique vision, the warmth and commitment of its people, and the untapped potential of this great historic movement. There was, and is, simply no other like it.

Every organization presents a face to the world. Most often that face belongs to the executive. I believe organizations are shaped by the people who run them and vice versa. Therefore, the first few chapters of this narrative are focused on the four executive directors who preceded me and my personal perspectives of key events which occurred during their tenure. These accounts are relatively brief. They are included in order to provide context for a longer story relating to the period 1981 through 2001 when I was Executive Director myself. A more comprehensive record of the period prior to 1981 can be found in Robert Egan's history of the community music school movement published in 1989 to mark the Guild's 50th anniversary.[1]

I am not a historian. I find it difficult to be completely objective about an association I ran for nearly one-third of its existence. By and large, the facts speak for themselves. But given my "inside" knowledge of the Guild, I inevitably developed a sort of 20-20 hindsight about things I did myself and what was done by those leaders who served the Guild so long and so well before and during my time. There were people I admired and trusted and those I did not. Likewise, others surely had mixed views about me. I have tried to be fair but I can only write this in my own voice with my own perspectives. In that way, it may be described as partly a history and partly a memoir. I ask that this chronicle be read in that light. I hope I will not offend but no doubt I will provoke opposing views. That is for a future historian to sort out. I have tried to tell it as I see it.

Lolita Mayadas,
Englewood, New Jersey
October 2020

Chapter One
Prologue

*We shall know our ends by our beginnings and
come to this place for the first time.*

– Bhagavad Gita

T
o provide context for this history of the Guild, it is perhaps
salutary to look back at the roots of the movement which gave
birth to the national association, as described in the following
quote from the Preface to Dr. Robert Egan's earlier history - Music
and the Arts in the Community: The Community Music School in
America.[1]

The United States of America can readily boast of its
contributions to the world of the arts and arts education.
Until the recent past, however, this country's
accomplishments in the arts have been underrated or
overlooked. Indeed this had been a nation recognized for
great achievements in exploring and settling new
territories, of emerging strongly during the Industrial
Revolution, and for the development and expansion of the
social settlement house movement begun in England
during the late nineteenth century.

From the last of the three came the idea that the arts of
musical performance and its related areas... should be
available to all regardless of age, nationality, or cultural or
religious background, and that no-one should be denied
music study for the want of the money to pay the cost of
instruction. The spark of inspiration caught fire in America

and spread throughout the land. So much so that musical instruction, in the lap of the social settlement houses became an important issue at national and international conferences of social work and other fields during the first quarter of the twentieth century.

The result of this was the formation of the community music school – an institution that offers music instruction of the highest quality for those who desire it, regardless of ability to pay.

This unique concept sparked the imagination of many settlement houses which then formed music divisions to serve the needs of an increasing number of European immigrants for whom music had always been an accepted part of their lives. An early example was Hull House in Chicago with Jane Addams at the helm. In 1922, the National Federation of Settlements created a Music Division, [2] which evolved into the National Guild of Community Schools of Music, which in turn became the National Guild of Community Schools of the Arts, the precursor to the National Guild for Community Arts Education of today, as described below.

The National Guild for Community Arts Education is the national service association for a diverse constituency of community-based institutions which provide high-quality instruction in the performing and visual arts for people of all ages, regardless of race, religion, aptitude or ability to pay. The purpose of the Guild is to foster, nurture, and encourage high quality arts education designed to meet community needs and to provide services and programs for the benefit of its members. As of 2001, those included institutional certification, technical assistance, advocacy, national and regional conferences, seminars and workshops, bi-monthly newsletters, and grants for special programs created in partnership with major national grant-makers.

* * * * *

In the folklore of the National Guild, Herbert Zipper is often considered to be its founder, an understandable but incorrect assumption since the organization was founded in 1937 by a small group of twelve settlement house music schools.[3] Herbert had an outsize impact on the organization but there were others before him who had served as executives. Prior to his appointment in 1967, the Guild had struggled for a way to turn a small group of like-minded community music schools into a functioning professional association. But in spite of years of effort, and the single-minded dedication of its leaders, the Guild remained a clubby group of sixteen institutions run by dedicated volunteers out of a peripatetic office.

Member schools shared a strong mission rooted in social service and a commitment to high quality music instruction for all. This was the glue that held them together and they proselytized about their cause as passionately as missionaries. Nevertheless, there was some grumbling in the ranks. More than ten years after its founding, the primary services provided by the Guild were the annual conference, a *Quarterly* newsletter, and little else. Some members began to question what services they were getting for their fees.

For years, the Guild depended almost entirely on membership dues – there was no cushion provided by grant income – and as a result fees had to be raised significantly to meet annual operating costs. This chicken and egg situation provoked a caustic letter from Maxwell Powers, Director of the Greenwich House Music School in New York: "We had hoped that the Guild would spearhead the thinking for community music schools all over the country. We had also hoped that there would be meaningful projects as a result of Guild affiliation...Unfortunately there has been no evidence of this fond hope. Added to the above, we received a bill which more than trebled our previous year's membership. Since the exorbitant membership fee is not included in our [school's] current operating budget, we are unable to meet this cost." [4]

"Exorbitant" membership fees might have been avoided if the Guild could have expanded its base of membership. However, the Guild's application procedures were burdensome and intimidating and must surely have discouraged many potential applicants. Moreover, in a misreading of the by-laws at the time, member schools were only accepted once a year at the Annual Meetings. And the application form was complex and voluminous, going so far as to request figures for all methods of transportation used by students to get to the school, including bicycles. Given this cumbersome process for admission, it is something of a miracle that there was any growth in membership at all. The process remained unchanged until the early eighties.

Spurred by intensive soul searching and the restiveness of some member schools in the early fifties, Board President, Howard Whittaker (Executive Director of the Cleveland Music School Settlement) drew up a ten-step Plan for the Future.[5] The first step was to hire an Executive-Secretary to look after the Guild's day-to-day affairs. Accordingly, Emily McCallip Adler was appointed to that position for the 1953-54 "season."[6] Emily was a former Director of the Cleveland Music School Settlement and a long-time member of the Guild's Executive Committee. There is no evidence that she was compensated for the job.

Following Emily's departure, a recommendation by Paul Freeman, Director of the David Hochstein Memorial Music School, led to the appointment of Alice Conway, a harpist and Hochstein faculty member, as Executive Secretary. An office was provided for her at the school at no cost to the Guild.[7] Alice took up her task with energy and enthusiasm. Her first objective was to get word of the Guild out to a broader audience. With that in mind, a publication was issued similar to the Quarterly (which had ceased publication in March 1947) with a new name – Guild Notes. And at the urging of Dr. Freeman, she also proposed a national performance contest for students of Guild schools to compete for awards to summer music camps.

In an attempt to get an objective and more comprehensive view of the needs of the field, the Board then decided to commission Dr. Max Kaplan, a well-known sociologist and musician, to carry out a survey of Guild schools. Entitled "National Guild of Community Music Schools: Observations and Recommendations," the report was duly presented on May 1, 1966 and circulated to the schools.

Twenty specific steps were proposed, divided into National and Internal segments. The recommendations spelled out six goals, all of which were adopted by the Guild in its strategic plans decades later, including:

- Conceive and organize a training program for administrators
- Redefine the membership
- Plan a national drive for funds with professional help
- Create new community schools
- Revitalize the Advisory Committee
- Plan and pursue a membership campaign

Dr. Kaplan closed with the words: "It is recommended that the present report be considered more as a plan for a plan than as a definitive set of recommendations."

The following year (1967), Alice was appointed Director of Hochstein. [8] It is likely that her new responsibilities consumed all her time and she gave up her Guild job at that point. She resigned from Hochstein in 1969 [9] and founded her own school in partnership with her husband, Thomas Barley. [10]

In 1967, Herbert Zipper, a Guild board member and former president, seized the initiative and approached the National Endowment for the Arts and the Rockefeller Foundation for funding to support a national office. And that is where this story begins....

Lolita Mayadas

Chapter Two
Grand Design

*The hopes for the future today are, in good share,
those of yesterday.*

– Richard Feynman[1]

For the first thirty years of its life, the National Guild of Community Music Schools led a nomadic existence, shuttling periodically between offices provided by board presidents at member schools from Cleveland to New York. Were it not for the heroic efforts of those early volunteer leaders, in particular Ruth Kemper, one-time Guild President, Janet Schenck, Founder-Director of the Manhattan School of Music, Johan Grolle of the Settlement Music School, and others, the National Guild must surely have passed into oblivion, remembered only as a footnote to the story of the settlement house movement. To Herbert Zipper, doing dual service as director of the Music Center of the North Shore[2] and President of the Guild's Board [1957-1961], and finally as its Executive Director, the situation was unacceptable. Never a man to think small, he had a vision of the Guild as a national, even global, force.

Herbert ran the organization with vision and flair for nearly five years and his passion, eloquence, and can-do spirit were an inspiration to all who knew him, at every level. He combined the fervor of the early leaders of the settlement house movement with an almost evangelistic message about the importance of music and the arts. If he had a flaw it was, perhaps, that his reach exceeded his grasp and some of his more ambitious projects literally fell apart under their own weight.[3] But his legacy was a host of innovative ideas and programs which provided the seeds and, in some cases, the templates for Guild initiatives developed decades after he left. Even today, he is widely remembered as the guiding spirit behind the start-up of new schools from Tennessee to Oregon. His oft-repeated mantra for the faint-hearted was: "Never give up; never give up; never, EVER, give up!"

I first heard about Herbert in India when I was running the Calcutta School of Music. I knew him to be a musician of repute, a survivor of the infamous concentration camps at Dachau and Manila and the pre-eminent expert in his field. I was advised to contact him by a friend at the American Consulate. In fact, I was so awed by his reputation that I did nothing. When I did meet him one afternoon at the Guild's 1982 conference I found him to be a man of great warmth and charm, with a demeanor as dapper as his appearance. I recognized him immediately from his photos as he walked toward me across an expanse of red and gold carpeting so typical of hotel banquet rooms. He was of medium height, with a slight stoop, an engaging smile and an intense, probing manner. He wasted no time on small talk but instead, after a gracious greeting, he launched immediately into an enthusiastic discourse about the potential of the Guild. I had been Executive Director of the Guild for just over a year. "You know, my dear," he said in his distinctive Austrian accent, "my wife, Trudl was about the same height as you are. She got a lot done in her life." He paused and looked at me with those bright, impish, black eyes, "It's always the women who get things done; but it's the little ones who are the strongest."

Herbert Zipper grew up in an affluent family in Vienna, the cultural center of Europe, where he and his family socialized with many of the leading writers and artists of his time. He went on to receive a Master's diploma from the Vienna State Academy [4] and embarked on a distinguished career as a composer, teacher, and conductor.

In 1938, the year of the Anschlüss, Herbert was arrested and sent to Dachau. Refusing to be cowed by the horrors of the camp, he decided to create a small orchestra using instruments made from stolen materials.[5] And every Sunday this make-shift group, inspired by Herbert's make-shift baton, met in an unused latrine to make music he wrote himself. This fervent mission to lift the spirits of the inmates through music also found voice through Herbert's song, "Dachau Lied," which eventually found its way into other camps. The piece was written together with Jura Soyfer, a co-prisoner and political journalist.[6] Following his incarceration at Dachau he was then sent to the Philippines.

Released in 1939 by the Japanese, Herbert returned to his vocation as a musician, becoming conductor of the Manila Symphony and Head of the Academy of Music. There, he married dancer Trudl Dubsky, and they emigrated to the United States in 1946, moving eventually to Illinois where Herbert took the job of Director at the Winnetka School of Music (now known as the Music Institute of Chicago). The school was co-founded by Richard D. Colburn, a successful businessman and amateur violist, along with two others. Together, they identified Herbert and hired him to run the school.[7] This was the beginning of a long and mutually fruitful friendship between Herbert and Richard.

"Herbert had this enduring belief in the humanizing effect of music and all the arts, and he early on established [a] bond with Dick Colburn," said Toby Mayman, the longtime President of the Colburn School.[8] That bond was passed down to the next generation. In fact, during an interview in 2018, Richard, one of Dick's sons, recalled with fondness his frequent visits as a youngster to Herbert and Trudl with his siblings. The children viewed the childless couple like family. Likewise, Herbert and Trudl were frequent visitors at the Colburn home.[9]

But little could anyone have guessed what a huge impact Herbert's friendship with Dick and the latter's munificence would have on the Guild and on USC's School of the Performing Arts in Los Angeles led by Grant Beglarian. That institution eventually morphed into the Colburn School, which is now one of the pre-eminent music schools in the country. "According to those who knew him," wrote

Claudia Luther in the *Los Angeles Times*, "the person who was a major influence on Colburn to use his wealth for music education was Herbert Zipper."[10]

Herbert was both seduced and challenged by the national footprint of the Guild, becoming active first as a Board member and then, in 1957 as President of the Board. Before all else, Herbert realized the Guild needed to get a national office, and a full-time director to run it. For this to happen he needed funds and he needed an imprimatur. The National Endowment for the Arts gave him both. Armed with their approval, he approached the Rockefeller Foundation where the Arts Department was headed by Norman Lloyd and later, the legendary Howard Klein.

from the desk of Herbert Zipper

With grants in hand from both sources,[11] Herbert promptly set up operations in 1967 at 626 Grove Street, Evanston, Illinois. That same year in a natural and logical move, the Board offered him the newly-created position of Executive Director. "I think there were something like 20 member schools," said Kal Novak many years later, "just a handful of schools."[12] The Guild's budget at the time was under $4,500 (about $35,000 in today's dollars).

Always inclined to look at the big picture, Herbert launched a series of major programs of grand design and scope. The most significant and enduring of these was a program developed in partnership with the University of California in 1974 to enable classroom teachers to practice the arts with their students on a daily basis. That initiative became a prototype for subsequent programs developed by the Guild decades later, such as the Arts Literacy Program in Newark Elementary Schools (ALPINES) and Partners in Excellence. Sadly, after a promising beginning, several programs such as those listed below, were eventually shelved for lack of funding or other reasons:

- The Mobile Academy of the Performing Arts in South East Arkansas, (Arkansas), a music education program launched in 1969 through a grant from ESEA Title I Funds.[13]

- A collaborative project with the New Orleans Symphony set up in 1969 to provide string instruction to elementary school children,[14] and

- The ambitious Arts for All Fund, launched at the Guild's Cleveland conference in 1970 with Arnold Gingrich, Chairman and Publisher of Esquire Magazine, as Chairman of the Fund [15] and a Board of Governors consisting of a blue-ribbon roster of prominent business leaders, some of whom (like Gingrich himself) were amateur musicians.[16]

To assist the Guild in the development of the Arts for All Fund, the governors voted unanimously to hire C.W. Shaver & Co.,[17] a leading fundraising and development consulting firm. Shaver was charged with carrying out a feasibility study provided the funds could be found to implement it. [18] Clearly, the Guild sought to broaden its base of support beyond the NEA and the Rockefeller Foundation. The Arts for All Fund seemed to provide a promising way to achieve that goal.

Given the dire situations the Guild faced in later years, and the great and endless struggles to raise even modest amounts of money, I mourn the demise of the Arts for All project which could have set the Guild on a wholly new and accelerated path to the future including service as advocate for its members. Why didn't it work? All the basic pieces were in place: a workable plan, a wealthy and influential board, a leading fundraiser, and a charismatic chief executive. Why then, did it not happen? Few of the players are still around and the reasons will never be known. This is one of those "what might have been" events that occur in the history of any institution, regretted but never effectively reprised.

Regardless of success or failure, few would deny the intrinsic merit of Herbert's ideas. But some controversy still remains over the relevance of the Guild's projects in the Far East (Manila, Bangkok, Taipei, and Seoul) to improve the study and performance of classical music in the Philippines especially at a time of scarce resources. Though supported by a separate grant from the JDR 3rd Fund, [19] those projects consumed a great deal of travel time and seemed to have only a tenuous connection to the Guild's central mission.

Herbert's approach to financial record-keeping at the Guild was somewhat quixotic. Needless to say, this presented a challenge for those brave souls on the Board who served as Treasurer.[20] Kal Novak, who held that position at that time, reported to the Board in May 1970 that, though the total balance of all funds appeared to be correct, his predecessor "did not keep any books" and he had to work backwards from check books, bank deposit books, cancelled checks, and funds received by him in order to determine the Guild's financial status. In doing so, Kal arrived at balances that [were] "widely different" from Herbert's figures as of October 31, 1969 and he could not reconcile them. At Kal's request, the Board willingly authorized him to hire a bookkeeper to "reconstruct the books for the past four years."

With the exponential increase in his activities, Herbert certainly had his hands full. He was managing projects in the pipeline, recruiting new members, traveling extensively, running several projects in the Far East, consulting, troubleshooting locally, administering the office, and cultivating potential funders all at the same time. [21] In addition, he was the go-to person for anyone, anywhere, who had an interest in starting a community music school. His can-do personality prompted him to take on every opportunity. But without adequate staff support, he was operating like the proverbial one-armed paper hanger. His heroic leadership style was exactly what the Guild needed at the time, but ultimately it was not sustainable.

Eventually, from weariness, frustration, or perhaps from his perpetual need to seek new horizons, Herbert decided to step down. "Although I had hoped for much greater progress," he wrote to members, "I believe the Guild is in better shape now than it was five years ago." [22]

The Board viewed Herbert's impending departure with stoic dismay. Their first practical step at Herbert's penultimate board meeting[23] was to parcel out some of his responsibilities to school directors through a new three-part regional structure: East, Middle, and West. Taking an optimistic view, Board President Harris Danziger pointed out that Herbert's departure, though a great loss, might well be a logical and positive step for the Guild and that the "division of labor may well have a strengthening effect." [24] The Board also expressed its gratitude to Herbert for his service, and added, "The Guild is indeed fortunate to have had a Director of his vision, scope, sophistication, and ability." A resolution commending him for his "fantastic efforts in the service of the Guild" passed unanimously. At the same meeting, an expense budget for $39,730 was approved, including a $27,800 line item for "Executive Director's Grant and Secretarial Services." [25]

The search for Herbert's successor was not undertaken by the Board. Instead, Herbert put forward the name of a friend and highly respected colleague, Charles C. Mark. He went on to list the unique qualities Charles would bring to the Guild especially in light of his work on the national scene. [26]

The Board trusted Herbert's judgment implicitly and promptly approved his recommended candidate. Invited to address his first meeting, Charles spoke about his "extreme interest" in the work of the Guild. He pointed out that though $150,000,000 had recently been expended by grantmakers nationally "in the name of the arts," the National Guild had received none of it. In his view he said, "The primary need is to make our case to...the public by communicating the facts and substance of our work more effectively."[27]

On the first Monday after the Board meeting, Herbert Zipper sent a letter to Guild members:

I have accepted the position of Project Director that was offered to me by the University of Southern California. Consequently, I will serve the Guild in my present capacity until July 1, 1972, when this office will move to Washington, D.C. During the past months the Guild's Executive Committee and I have worked out most of the details for a smooth transfer of responsibilities of this office. Of course I will participate in Guild matters in the future as much as my time will allow me, but for the Guild's future as well as for mine, a new beginning promises to keep us from growing old, and therefore we all should look upon this change as a new and welcome challenge.

Charles C. Mark has a master's degree in social work. He was the first Executive Director of the Winston-Salem Arts Council; the Founding Director of the Arts and Education Council of St. Louis; Arts Consultant to the White House; Director of State and Community Operations and Director of Planning and Analysis of the National Endowment for the Arts; President of the Performing Arts Council of the Los Angeles Music Center; and, since 1970, Publisher of the Arts Reporting Service [a bi-weekly newsletter covering the international arts world].

There is no better man in America for the Guild.

In spite of his imminent departure, Herbert was still thinking out of the box. At his last board meeting,[28] the agenda included a review of several programs in the planning phase: a program to provide scholarships to disadvantaged minority students, a project to place a string quartet in residence in Bangkok, and a proposal to engage regional school directors in the Guild's new "division of labor" initiative. He also presented a report on a proposal to develop an objective study on the effect of a music-oriented primary education on early childhood learning. A $25,000 grant request had been submitted to "a major national foundation." At Herbert's request, three committees were immediately appointed to lead the project. This was done so that the Guild could be prepared in case the grant was approved.

Also left on the table was a slew of new proposals which were approved by the Board over the years but never executed. "He was a grand soul," said Kal Novak, "but he had big plans which did not always work out in practice."[29]

> *Herbert's creative muse remained alive and well throughout his life. His dreams were not minor. Many years later at an annual conference he asked me for a few minutes at the microphone. He didn't tell me why and I didn't ask. Everyone knew who he was and he got a great round of applause. Then he launched into a passionate case for the Guild to set up a nationwide Arts Corps to encourage faculty members to teach disadvantaged youngsters in rural locations. He wanted this modeled on the Peace Corps.*

Four months later, at a meeting of member schools in Boston on May 1st, Herbert presented his final report prefaced with a summary of his four and one-half years. He began by urging Guild members to keep foremost in their minds the importance of their work as a national organization and to think of themselves as more than just leaders of their own schools, but rather as contributors to a national movement in the education of the young. His remarks resonated with a group that was made up primarily of school directors and he received a standing ovation.[30]

At the time, member schools numbered 45,[31] a two-fold increase since the start of Herbert's tenure. Herbert had also succeeded in obtaining recurring annual operating grants from the National Endowment for the Arts – no mean feat in an increasingly competitive environment. Many decades later, Board member Richard Casper was to speak of his "keen sense of loss," a sentiment that must surely have been shared by all. [32] It was a tough environment for Charles Mark to step into.

Whatever he felt privately about Herbert's departure, Harris Danziger was upbeat in his letter to the membership: [33]

> Finding Charles Mark for the position of Executive Director was a real break. "Chuck" for many years has been a most powerful spokesman for the Arts, both within and outside governmental agencies. His energy is matched by a vision akin to our own. He will coordinate the work of the regional bodies and, above all, work on the Arts for All Fund. I know that Herbert will not want any expression of sorrow at this time. Yet those of us who have worked with him may be permitted to say that we will deeply miss his inspiring closeness. (We will even miss those midnight telephone calls.) Above all, we will miss the constant example of an all too rare breed: the Artist as a Total Man. So... a new era begins. I know we will measure up to its demands.

In this atmosphere of genial optimism and goodwill, tempered with anxiety at the passing of the torch, Chuck Mark moved the Guild's office in June 1972 to his home at 9214 Three Oaks Drive, Silver Spring, Maryland.

Chapter Three
A New Era Begins

Between the concept and the creation falls the shadow.

– T.S. Eliot[1]

An affable and erudite man, Charles C. Mark came to the Guild with an impressive set of credentials as a writer, communicator, and policy wonk. He had served as a consultant to the White House, helped establish the NEA, directed the NEA's state and community operations, and explored the feasibility of states creating their own arts agencies. In addition, he had written news briefs on the arts for National Public Radio, taught cultural history at George Washington University and American University, and developed the Arts Reporting Service newsletter – a must-read for arts administrators. Having spent more than 40 years in the arts, there was no doubt about his deep commitment to his chosen field. Further, he was a true believer in the Guild, and he had made a strong pitch in his newsletter for support from NEA's new Expansion Arts Program.[2]

But in spite of his national stature, it is unclear why he was offered the job of executive director of the Guild in the first place or, in fact, why he accepted it. Except for a brief stint as president of the Los Angeles Music Center, he had little management or fundraising experience and no experience working for a community music school. He was known as a thinker, rather than a manager. He would have been ideal as a Guild advocate. Be that as it may, the Board hired him without demur, relieved at the smoothness of the transition.

A prolific writer, Chuck's work included a novel, plays, poems, articles, and opinions about many of the major issues in the arts. Many were published in major national newspapers and journals. His undated *Sonnet for a Fallen Philanthropist* published on his website after his death in 1998 could well have reflected his frame of mind when he stepped into Herbert Zipper's shoes at the Guild.

When leaders of great vision die who takes their place?
Who brings inspired light to hold the unenlightened souls
in line and makes the timid follower stand tall and bold?

When visionaries die who holds the key to all those locks
that make the doors appear to open with a magic touch?
Are we the heirs to visions we don't know are here?

"It is difficult to know how to start communication with all of you," he wrote to the member schools in early September 1972, "since some of you I don't know at all and some I know only slightly. But let me begin by saying that I will be as open and informative about the activities of the Guild as is humanly possible, leaning perhaps toward the prudent to avoid raising hopes unnecessarily."[3] He went on to report on two grants from the National Endowment for the Arts: the first a pending proposal for $17,500 toward the operation of the Guild offices. "This grant," he wrote, "has become virtually an annual occurrence and testifies to the confidence which the NEA has in our work. Matching funds, over and above the usual important income from dues, is now being sought. The prognosis is good."

Another non-matching grant of $45,000, also from the NEA, was said to be in the "last stages of approval." The grant was to be used "to provide direct fund raising and management counseling to member schools." The funds requested represented just 50% of "the total needed to provide first quality services for one year." [4] Chuck also confirmed that C.W. Shaver and Co. had been "tentatively" engaged to continue serving as the Guild's research and development counsel.

While this grant was intended to support services to the
field, it would, in effect, double the Guild's annual

operating budget. Obviously, a compelling case had been made. But seen from the standpoint of exhausted grant seekers in later years who struggled to get a piece of the shrinking pie at the NEA, it seemed so simple at the time. We used to joke that all you had to do was to buttonhole someone in the elevator and you got funded. No doubt this is apocryphal but in those days, not long after the NEA was established, money seemed plentiful and the competition a lot less daunting than in the nineties and beyond.

"Lolita gives readers a glimpse of the early NEA days in the 1970's, that most of today's arts leaders have not experienced," wrote Scott Shanklin-Peterson, Former Senior Deputy Chairman, National Endowment for the Arts, in an email dated June 17, 2020. "With fewer arts organizations, less competition for NEA funding and a more nimble federal government in the 1970's, struggling organizations often looked to the NEA for a quick "elevator grant" as some jokingly called them, just to "keep the lights on," for another year - a sharp contrast to today's procedures."

In fact, the consistent and generous support of the NEA from 1967 onwards did indeed "keep the lights on" for the Guild for several decades. Their grants were critical to the Guild's survival and to its ability to provide ever-expanding services to the field. Further, the NEA's seal of approval was eminently reassuring to other private funders (too numerous to list here) who also gave us grants, both large and small, through the years. The largest of these was the Wallace Funds. On behalf of the Guild, I offer all of them our profound thanks for their confidence in the Guild and, thereby, the entire field of community arts education.

Carl Shaver took on his task with relish, assisted in large measure by the approval of the NEA non-matching grant[5] and the potential of a distinguished board of governors headed by Arnold

19

Gingrich, Chairman and Publisher of Esquire magazine. Always methodical, Carl started from the ground up: first, his firm carried out nineteen visits [6] to community schools to develop a case study; second, he presented four regional workshops for school administrators and board members around the country (attended by 118 individuals); [7] third, he provided technical assistance to at least seven schools and fourth, he prepared a comprehensive manual on fundraising and financial administration which became a veritable text-book for member schools for years to come.[8] Halsey North, a senior associate in his firm at the time remembers: "I think the hallmark of the firm was Carl's unique emphasis on financial organization and reporting and plans. Confidence comes in the details is the phrase we use." [9]

At the Annual Meeting in November 1972, Carl briefly summarized the findings of his visits to member schools:

1. A strong case for funding Community Music Schools can be made.

2. The need for funds is reaching crisis proportions.

3. The administration of many schools is inadequate.

4. There is a need for improvement in the quality of voluntary boards of the schools.

5. There is a need to dramatize the importance of music education, the Community Music School, and the Guild to society at large.

6. The 10-year development plan originally established must be shortened and financial goals changed.

On the topic of fundraising, Carl listed four essential ingredients including the "capacity and resources" of the Board of Trustees. No doubt heads nodded in agreement around the table. All school directors expect their own boards to raise money. But by the same token, their own fundraising responsibility as Guild Trustees was never discussed. Instead, in recognition of personal financial constraints, the Board began working on a policy of reimbursement for board travel to "required" meetings. [10]

At the same time, the Board unanimously accepted Carl's recommendation that the size of the board be increased to include influential lay leaders from the Arts for All Board. [11] Chuck Mark remarked that the larger Board would give the Guild a national base from which to carry on a national fundraising campaign. And Sol Schoenbach, Executive Director of the Settlement Music School in Philadelphia and a Guild Trustee, suggested building a pool of prospects based on recommendations from member schools. The enthusiasm was real but it did not last. It would be a decade or more before the critical issues of board responsibilities and board development were addressed again in any meaningful way.

Meantime, Chuck was operating under an expansive mandate from the board "to assume full responsibility for the direction of the Guild," [12] a charge so broad it could be interpreted any number of ways. Since specific job responsibilities had not been spelled out, he took a broad-brush approach to his job, developing a series of three scholarly, if somewhat didactic, Position Papers which laid out the Guild's possible expansion into a broader spectrum of the arts, the issue of fundraising for the field as a whole, and potential services to the field.

To provide context, Chuck drafted what he called Background Materials as a preface to each Position Paper. An excerpt from the Third Paper reads:

> Two concepts of programming are obvious. One method is to estimate the amount of funds available for a given period and tailor the program to fit the dollars. The other method is to examine the needs of constituents and somehow find the funds necessary to carry out the desired program. The former produces a calm and satisfied executive and Board, but a membership which is frustrated. The latter produces an uneasy executive and Board, but a reasonably satisfied membership. The sensible course to follow is one which strives to satisfy needs, but which avoids over-commitment to services beyond financial ability. To date, the Guild has followed this course with a service emphasis on the organization of

new schools and a general broadening of influence for the community school movement.[13]

To spur further discussion about program priorities, five questions were presented to the membership at the 1972 conference. The questions are paraphrased below:

1. Does the membership consider it to be highly desirable for C.W. Shaver Company to provide fund raising and management counseling services on a long-term basis?

2. Is it worth it to continue the administration of the Music Performance Trust Fund grant[14] in spite of the inordinate paper work?

3. Would an organized personnel placement service be helpful?

4. Is an intern program desirable within member schools?

5. Would there be a benefit to newer directors to hold administrative workshops?

Presumably, these questions were distributed to members, but no decisions were made about program choices, content or funding.

With a little tweaking, Chuck's Position Papers could have provided an effective introduction to a strategic plan. Instead, they may have unwittingly played into the Guild's tendency in those days to indulge in fevered soul-searching at times of crisis – something I experienced several times during my own tenure: Who are we? What are we about? Where are we headed? What should we be doing? But existentialist questions such as these were a distraction the Guild could little afford. It was running out of money and time. Urgent action was needed to keep the Guild afloat. But no such action was taken.

That said, one major accomplishment was the approval of a name change for the Guild that would encompass the other arts – a positive and forward-thinking move reflecting the increasing number of multi-arts member schools. [15] The new name was to be National

Guild of Community Schools of Music and the Arts. A set of revised membership criteria[16] was drawn up by a specially constituted Task Force[17] and approved by the Board and membership on May 21, 1973. These criteria formed the bedrock principles for institutional membership for decades to come. Little could the Board have known how dire the consequences of diversification into the other arts would be for NEA funding in the immediate future.

With the formulation of his Position Papers, Chuck was looking for a way to educate and engage the board and membership and to build consensus. To his credit, he spent many months developing these essays, but in the end, members were at a loss as to what to do with them. But without firm leadership and direction about the path forward, the Board migrated to more familiar ground: extensive discussions about the proposed change of name, membership requirements, employee benefits, pension plans, group life insurance, Board travel reimbursement, and program design. [18] The Arts for All Fund, left untended, foundered on the shoals of all this busy activity.

Meantime, the clock was ticking.

By the spring of 1973, the Guild found itself with just $6,000 in cash and receivables in hand. [19] Except for a new proposal to the Rockefeller Brothers Fund and two pending applications to the NEA, there were no other likely funding prospects in the pipeline.

Faced with a situation he could neither control nor improve, Chuck decided to step down.

"I wish some good news could be reported at this time, but....no funds have been available for any activities since July 1 and my time has necessarily been spent pursuing other means of income. As a result of these efforts it has become necessary for me to submit my resignation as of November 1." [20]

Chuck was popular with the Board and many were sorry to see him go. "He was a great thinker and a very sympathetic person," said Kal Novak. "Everyone liked him. I liked him very much." [21]

Helpful as always, Carl Shaver offered free office space and either full-time or part-time services in view of the "financial crisis" facing the Guild to "help advance the cause of the National Guild and

23

its member schools." [22] His position was that he would accept no more money until the national office was firmly established. [23] From that time on, he would receive no payments against his invoices. Eventually, he just tore them up. [24]

Eight years later, soon after I became executive director, I went to see Carl in his office. I knew the Guild owed him nearly $20,000, [25] and I was prepared for a cool reception. But he greeted me with characteristic grace. I asked if he would be prepared to write a monthly article on fundraising for our newsletter. In response, he immediately summoned Halsey North, a senior associate at his firm, and instructed him to give me what I wanted (on a pro bono basis). Halsey had no choice but his was a generous nature and he readily complied. I believe he too had caught the Guild bug for he frequently donated his time as a conference presenter for years afterward. He used to joke that whenever he heard my voice on the phone, he knew he was going to end up volunteering for something! [26]

In short order, the Guild moved out of Chuck's house and into Carl Shaver's offices at 654 Madison Avenue in New York. [27]

"[Carl] had a large office and two little side offices through another door and...those side offices [were] the headquarters of the Guild," said Halsey. "At one point [he] paid the executive director's salary when the Guild was having financial problems. I think the relationship with the Guild was very different than any other he had. I think it was a real soft spot in his heart because he understood what it meant to the lives of children and young people." [28]

Chapter Four
A Parting of the Ways

When you come to a fork in the road, take it.

– Yogi Berra[1]

T he Board was not accustomed to a situation like this. It had never before been called upon to search for an executive director, knowing only Herbert Zipper, their one-time president, who had created the position, raised the funds, secured office space, and then taken on the job himself, to the relief of all concerned. And when the time came, he presented his hand-picked successor to the Board which accepted his choice without reservation. But now, Herbert was gone and Chuck Mark, too, was leaving.

This was the first major crisis the Board had to resolve on their own, although it would not be the last. Led by Board President Dorothy Maynor, they convened a meeting in September 1973 to consider their options. Someone suggested that an executive director "may not be necessary" and that the Guild could operate temporarily with a secretary using school executives as consultants. Attending as a guest, Carl Shaver was not impressed, pointing out that the Guild needed "someone of distinction and position to carry on the work of the Guild and to seek funding." Accordingly, a search committee was formed, headed by Howard Whittaker, to draw up criteria and carry out the search.[2]

Before the fall had turned to winter, Dorothy Amarandos was in place as the new executive director.[3] The decision by the Board was unanimous. Educated at the Eastman School of Music, Dorothy was known as a performing artist and teacher, having served as a long-time

25

member of the Rochester Philharmonic under Erich Leinsdorf and as principal cellist of the Columbus Symphony. She was also professor of cello at Ohio State University as well as Denison University, Ohio Wesleyan University, and Otterbein College. Aside from her musical accomplishments, she also had the vision and energy to start and maintain new organizations such as Ars Antiqua, a Renaissance music-drama group and later, Cello Speaks, a series of one-week cello workshops for adults. It is likely that her organizational skills as an entrepreneur brought her to the attention of the Michigan Council for the Arts where she was appointed Coordinator of the Performing Arts Program.

Three months after Dorothy was hired, she presented a contract letter to the Executive Committee setting out her own responsibilities. [4] It was accepted without amendments or lengthy discussion. The list is daunting to say the least. It "included but [was] not limited to" the following:

1. Define immediate, intermediate and long-range objectives of the National Guild and present them to the Board of Directors for consideration and action.

2. Pay periodic visits to member schools and ...counsel with (sic) School Directors and/or their Boards of Trustees.

3. Develop and maintain a resource file of professional personnel as a service to member schools.

4. Assist in the development of new member schools and new services in existing institutions.

5. Assist in the establishment of criteria and artistic standards of teaching at the various grade levels.

6. Organize and prepare an annual conference and other meetings of the Guild, including Board of Directors meetings and Executive Committee meetings.

7. Represent the Guild at meetings of other national organizations when deemed appropriate for the development of the Guild and to provide information for the Executive Director.

8. Administer and maintain accounting procedures for all grants, contributions and revenues.

These expectations could best be described as a triumph of hope over reality. The Board had transitioned from the broadest possible mandate for Chuck Mark to an itemized laundry list of tasks that would have tested even Herbert Zipper's prodigious energies.

When I asked Dorothy during an interview in the fall of 2006 how she could possibly have accepted this document, she said she probably wrote it herself. I was surprised. "But you would have had to work 72 hours a day!" I said. "You were only one person!" "But that's exactly what I did, my dear," she responded. "That's exactly what I did."

As a new hire, Dorothy was not familiar with the inner workings of the Guild, and she prudently asked for priorities for the next six months. In response, the Executive Committee noted that "the general thrust of the Executive Office should be to insure its own existence...and [to]...demonstrate what the product is." [5] Consequently, the following four tasks were selected without elaboration:

1. Brochure [6]

2. Funding for next year

3. Carry out programs

4. Jack up funding

The Board also asked Dorothy to speak with Chuck Mark "at length" and to contact some of the foundations he had approached.

"Dorothy Amarandos walked into a hotbed when she accepted the position," wrote Robert Egan, author of the Guild's first history and one-time Guild President. [7] and in fact, her prior experience could barely have prepared her for the unique challenges she faced at the Guild. First, there was confusion about the division of responsibilities between the Executive Director and the Board, and second, the Guild had become increasingly dependent on the National Endowment for the Arts to finance its day-to-day operations. And third, financial projections were tortuous, to say the least. The budget was split four ways: the Far East projects budget, the Arts for All Fund budget, the Guild budget, and the "executive office" budget. Project funding was forthcoming from the JDR 3rd Fund and the National Endowment for the Arts. At the same meeting where Dorothy was hired, the Treasurer reported that "the Guild budget is relatively stable and can be prepared very simply. The executive office budget is more flexible and is dependent upon grants and special funds." [8] Not surprisingly, in Dorothy's opinion these interrelated budgets were a "total mystery." [9] Further, while earned revenue goals from membership dues were spelled out, line items for grants and contributions were missing entirely from the operating budget statements. The issue of contributed revenue is referenced just once in the Board's list of priorities to "jack up funding."

Of course it wasn't as simple as that. As Carl Shaver had pointed out, "Funds for a national office are difficult to raise and ... attention should be focused on expansion and program development." [10]

At the time the Guild's core programs and services were minimal. When I asked Dorothy years later what the Guild did for its schools, she responded: "The Guild was supposed to be supporting the schools and increasing the number of schools and making [it possible for] the schools ...to run. And we had surveys and panel discussions about what the schools accomplished in their community and that sort of thing. But all this came as a result of the National Guild being a clearinghouse of ideas and data." [11]

This menu of services had few takers. The Guild had built no history of funding with any private foundations save the Rockefeller Foundation and, given the dearth of fundable programs, new prospects were few. Even Dorothy's meeting with Chuck Mark yielded no concrete sources.

Dorothy complained later that Carl Shaver did not do enough to raise funds. But as Carl repeatedly reminded Dorothy. [12] "In order for us to be effective in assisting the... National Guild in securing gifts and grants, certain elements must be present. One of these is an effective program of services to existing member schools. Obviously, if you can put the Guild in a position where the number of potential new schools would be 20 or 30 it would lend tremendous strength to funding requests and multiply many times the opportunity of securing important money."

In that context, Carl also endorsed the idea of an internship program for potential school directors. He noted, "To this date nothing exists in the way of a specific formal program which can be used in seeking gifts and grants for this purpose." [13]

The need to raise funds could not have been more urgent. But there was no agreement on the tactics. Instead, differences between Carl and Dorothy about respective job responsibilities continued to surface. By mid-March, tensions had escalated to the point that Carl thought it wiser to withdraw.

"We recognize," he wrote to Dorothy, [14] "that you assumed your position only two months ago, and that you have been faced with many problems. We are sensitive to the problems which confront you in your new task, and wish to be as helpful as we can." He added, "It is our feeling that at this particular moment the Shaver Company has not been able to be as effective as we would like to be and cannot be as effective as we believe we must until such time as the [National Guild] has progressed to a point where we have sufficient definite programs to enable us to help the Guild [to] secure gifts and grants." He therefore offered to cancel his company's contractual services to the national office and eliminate his contractual monthly fee. The counseling services to member schools would remain unchanged. Concluding on a more hopeful note, he added, "We are prepared to reassume a vigorous role as fund-raising counsel for the National Office at a time when it appears that the ingredients for your success are present."

Dorothy responded with a rebuttal.[15] She asserted that many of the key duties he allocated to the Guild were, in fact, to be shared with C.W. Shaver, a position diametrically opposed to Carl's.

Not surprisingly, the relationship between them was rapidly breaking down. Each felt the other had dropped the ball in terms of job responsibilities. Ultimately, Carl felt compelled to write to the Guild's President, Dorothy Maynor, founder of the Harlem School of the Arts on March 26th, "We have not found our relationship with Mrs. Amarandos to be satisfactory. We are sympathetic to the extremely difficult situation which confronts her and have wished to help as much as possible." However, citing specific issues, he confirmed his intent to withdraw from any formal arrangements and to serve "simply as a friend of the Guild." [16]

Carl's letter to Dorothy Maynor was shared with the Executive Committee and, presumably, the Board. But they could do little to rectify the situation.

Two days later, on March 28th, [17] the Executive Committee recorded its gratitude and "that of the entire National Guild" to Carl Shaver and his staff for the "enormous help" received from them in the past.

At the time, the Board was made up of a majority of school directors who could provide little help in terms of national foundation contacts or sustenance from personal resources. If it is true that the attributes of an ideal board are Work, Wisdom, and Wealth, the Guild possessed a surfeit of wisdom and work but, except in rare cases, no wealth at all. The Board, as constituted, was simply not capable of raising funds for the Guild, nor was it set up to open doors.

In spite of Carl's urgent call for the Guild to identify and recruit persons of "distinction, leadership and means" to fill certain places on the Board of Trustees, the effort had yielded no results. He himself had submitted 51 names and the Board had come up with 16 names of school trustees, plus 7 at-large nominations, some taken from the Arts for All Board of Governors.[18] Carl firmly believed that the lack of progress on this count had seriously impeded the Guild's ability to build a base of wealthy and influential supporters and a network of connections to grant makers.

Dorothy's own opinion of the Board was direct and uncompromising: "The Guild was only a directors' club. It was not a national force. The fact that the board was made up of school directors seemed a problem to me and I wanted to get some people on the board who were not school directors." [19]

The Guild's cash situation was becoming more precarious by the day. Responding to an urgent appeal to member schools, Dorothy Maynor generously arranged for a short-term loan of $5,000 from the Harlem School of the Arts to tide the Guild over. "We can only hope," wrote Amarandos, "that we will not be in such a tight situation again." [20] Shortly thereafter, the NEA saved the day yet again with an installment payment of $25,600.

In July 1974, Carl Shaver asked Dorothy to move out of his offices, ostensibly because of staff increases at his firm. The Guild again relocated to a new space at 200 West 57th Street, outfitted this time with borrowed furniture from Dorothy's basement. [21]

Contemporary reviews of Dorothy's tenure at the Guild suggest that there were successes as well as disappointments. On the plus side, she could legitimately chalk up several key areas of achievement. Her eloquently written account of the conference in May 1974, hosted by Richard Casper and the Cape Cod Conservatory, makes for inspiring reading even today, and speaks to the quality and effectiveness of the event. According to Dick Casper, the success of the event was due in no small part to her efforts. The conference prompted Dorothy Maynor to wax poetic at a board meeting: "The Guild has embarked on an exciting journey and at last the doors are open to the sister arts. The National Guild will blaze new frontiers with its message: Every boy and girl should share in the beauty of the arts. We, the Guild, must prayerfully pursue this mission of beauty for our children." [22]

Dorothy Amarandos had also addressed a host of key administrative issues. She updated and formalized the Code of Regulations, revised membership standards, created a regional chapter structure, drafted a new statement of purpose and objectives, developed a long-range membership and fundraising plan, and created an internship program which debuted in September 1976 with Marcy Horwitz as Project Coordinator. [23] She had begun to address board development issues and she personally tried to recruit members of the erstwhile Arts for All Fund for the Board. She was also involved in a new Joint Committee with the National Association of Schools of Music to foster cooperation between the two groups, particularly with respect to standards for prep divisions [24] and the awarding of Guild certificates to outstanding secondary age music students, [25] a program initially proposed by Allen Sapp, Dean of the University of Cincinnati College Conservatory of Music and a Guild Trustee, to recognize outstanding achievers at each participating member school. [26] What she did not, or perhaps could not, do is to build relationships with her constituents. Nor were her antennae out for signs of trouble.

By October 1974, with no monies coming in to the Guild's coffers, Dorothy was both frustrated and desperate. She wrote to the Board:

> The largest worry is that we still have no matching funds.... The application to ITT was turned down unequivocally for this year – as has been every other foundation and corporation so far. More serious is our lack of a well-honed plan of services – and of course I'm unable to conduct programs and services until we have the money to do so. I feel that our potential is very great, that good timing is on our side, that we have one whale of a story to tell, but I NEED HELP to find survival money. What do you suggest?

The Board's response a month later was to adopt a budget that included a timely and significant increase in earned revenue from school dues. Unlike fundraising, this was an area where the Board could, and did, help out. That month, Membership Chairman Sol Schoenbach reported to the Board that four schools had been admitted to membership and another eight were in the pipeline. [27] But then the Board got a little carried away. With more zest than realism, they set an ambitious target that would double the membership from 50 to 100 schools in twelve months and double it again the following year. [28]

Three months later [29] Dorothy sent another *cri de coeur* to the Board:

> It may have seemed to you that I should be able to sustain the Guild, develop the programs, and find the support monies all by myself – but this is definitely not the case! Since you are my Board of Governors, I need your help, your input and especially your communications.

But there was no quick fix. Clearly, the situation was going from bad to worse and internal dissensions were growing. A plan for reorganization was floated and gained some traction. By mid-1975, circumstances were serious enough that a new and more aggressive Acting Board President, Kenneth Wendrich, decided to take matters in hand. A 3-day meeting of the Executive Committee was convened to discuss the state of the Guild and future strategies. While recognizing Dorothy's legitimate concerns about the Board, the Committee also noted the "implied" dissatisfactions expressed by school directors about her administrative style and their concerns about an Executive Office "which does not serve its constituency in any meaningful way."[30]

Dorothy had worked long and hard, but in the end she became a polarizing figure, unable to retain the support of the Board or the membership as a whole. By the time the 1976 Washington conference ended in November, the Board had decided to let her go. A pink slip or letter of dismissal would be heartless. Instead, three Board members, including Lester Glick, the new Board President, flew down to New York to meet with Dorothy personally. When the meeting ended, she opened her office door, said goodbye to her staff, and walked out. Years later, she recalled how deeply hurt and unappreciated she felt for all the work she had done under difficult circumstances.[31]

Looking back on a turbulent time, Richard Casper, Executive Director of the Cape Cod Conservatory and a Board member, offered some perspectives of his own: "Dorothy was much more of a victim than a lightning rod. And yes, there were a great deal of questions like: What can the Guild do for me? Why are we spending all this money on a national office and director? My school doesn't need it… and so on. There was a great deal of divisiveness. Some of it was self-serving but some of it was about a simple conflicting vision. There were perfectly legitimate disagreements. But at that time in Washington, the personal differences became more evident than the philosophical and theoretical."[32]

When asked in 2006 what her legacy was, Dorothy said, "I would …think that my aim and my attempt was to nationalize the Guild [in order] to give it a sense of direction and purpose and mission and to get it to be recognized as a national force. I didn't succeed entirely but that was my goal."[33]

Chapter Five
Turning Point

Nothing endures but change

— Heraclitus[1]

"By the time the conference started, there was revolution in the air," remembers Marcy Horwitz, who was in Washington to help staff the 1976 conference. "Dorothy really did come under attack. She was always complaining, rightly or wrongly, that there wasn't any money."[2]

Quite coincidentally, the Washington Conference was the first Guild conference I attended. At the time I was Registrar and Dean of Students at the David Hochstein Music School and Helen Tuntland (Jackson), the school's charismatic Executive Director, signed me up to go with her. She thought I might enjoy it and learn something from my peers. I remember it vividly for no other reason except that I don't remember anything at all. Nothing and everything seemed to be going on. I do recall coming across small knots of people with their heads together buried in intense conversation and Helen being pulled hither and thither for this or that meeting. She asked me to go with her to the Annual Meeting. But that's it. I also recall being introduced to Dorothy Amarandos very briefly while she was in transit from one session to another, but there was no time for anything more than a brief greeting.

"For three and a half days," said Marcy later, "things were falling through the cracks. I was just trying to figure out where the next hole in the dike was. In many ways it was exhilarating, but in the way a total chaotic event is. The Board was aware of what was going on." [3] Fortunately, Marcy could count on Sandra Kaplan, who had been hired to help with the conference. She eventually stayed on for six years as Marcy's assistant.

At the end of one particularly hectic day, Marcy recalled, "I had been working all day long. At about 9:00 o'clock I went down to the coffee shop at the hotel and ordered a salad and a glass of wine. I was exhausted and feeling really out of control. Lester Glick [President of the Guild's Board] walked in and asked if he could join me. 'Sure,' I said. He sat down and I said, 'Lester, I just have to tell you – when we get back to New York, I'm going to clean up after the conference and then I think I'm going to need to resign.' And he said, 'I'm going to ask you not to do that." I asked him why. He said again, 'I'm just going to ask you not to do that.' "

Later, at the New York office on the day Dorothy was asked to leave, Lester Glick and Board members Monroe Levin and Helen Tuntland invited Marcy to be Interim Director until a new search could be organized. Buoyant as always, Marcy's first thought was, "Well, cool, I can do that!"

Marcy's personality was as different from Dorothy's as chalk is to cheese.

Marcy Horwitz was born in Brooklyn, but for most of her young life, her family was continually on the move, spending time in South Florida, Long Island, and the US Virgin Islands. During one two-year stint when they lived in Rego Park, Queens, she signed up for piano lessons at the Third Street Music School in lower Manhattan. That experience helped strengthen an early and ongoing interest in musical studies, and she went on to Clark University in Worcester, Massachusetts, from where she graduated with a B.A. in music. Her first job was teaching Orff and Kodaly at the newly founded Worcester Community School in Massachusetts where she was also hired to work in the office on registrations. Within a short while, she was appointed Acting Director. She was just 23 years of age. "I don't remember being afraid," she said. "I was proud of myself!" Though she continued to work at the school even after John Cox was hired as permanent Director, she eventually decided to spread her wings and joined the public relations department at the Hartt School of Music College Division in Hartford, Connecticut. At that time, Robert (Bob) Christensen was running the Hartt Community Music School.

One warm summer's day in 1976, she found herself on the bus to New York with Bob, who was escorting some music school kids on a field trip to the City. They did a lot of talking. At Bob's suggestion, she casually dropped by the National Guild to see Dorothy Amarandos. To her great surprise, she was hired on the spot to run the Internship Program. Like almost everyone else, Dorothy was very taken by Marcy: "She was a very outgoing, charming young woman. She seemed to be very bright." [4]

Under Marcy's upbeat, efficient direction as Interim Director, the Guild gradually reverted to a state of normalcy and calm. Six months after the Washington conference she was commended for her efforts. Tellingly, the search for a new Executive Director was tabled. [5] In the words of Dick Casper, "Marcy brought peace. She was smart and capable and she was too young to threaten and annoy people. "[6] But there was work to be done.

Since frugality was the order of the day, the Guild began to explore the possibility of shared office space, eventually finding compatible facilities at the Associated Council for the Arts, 570 Seventh Avenue, New York. Marcy reported that there was one large "double" room with a receptionist thrown in at no charge. The rent was $250 a month – which translated to an estimated saving of about $1,200/year. With the approval of the Board, the Guild moved into its new premises on September 1977.

Under more settled, even optimistic, conditions, Lester and Marcy made their respective reports at the Annual Meeting in San Francisco in 1977. For her part, Marcy explained that the Guild's primary focus for the past year had been on strengthening services to the field in the following categories: Education, Advocacy, Research, and Communications.

Lester Glick followed with his perspectives of events over the last twelve months: "The year 1976 was spent largely in rehashing old problems, trying to bring about some cohesiveness, and attempting to obtain advice and counsel from a number of experts, some of whom were Board members." Lester then outlined the process that resulted in the termination of Dorothy's services and the hiring of Marcy, first as Interim Director, then as Acting Director, and finally as Executive Director in September 1977. He was fulsome in his praise. "It is largely because of the commitment and devotion of two young women, Marcy Horwitz and Sandie Kaplan, her part-time assistant, and the renewed interest of a revitalized Board of Trustees that the National Guild has survived and can look forward to a brighter future." He added that there would be two areas of concentration in the coming year: fundraising for specific programs and membership development. Regarding services to members, he stressed that "as we obtain more funds, services will increase." [7]

Having set its own house in order, the Guild began to look for ways to expand its sphere of influence (otherwise known as advocacy) and to have a voice in the development of arts education policy. In order to achieve these goals, a four-pronged approach emerged: first, to develop partnerships with other national associations; second, to testify at state and federal public hearings; third, to achieve greater visibility by placing or promoting articles in other national association journals; and fourth, to participate in major arts education forums. In short, the Guild wanted a seat at the table and an office in Washington was considered essential. "Dorothy [had] engaged Ernest Dyson, who was running a small school in the inner city, to be our [representative] in Washington," said Marcy. "He was active in community arts in DC. He had real street cred, real street smarts. I wasn't in a position to have evaluated how well he was doing his job but it felt good to have those connections in DC." [8]

Ernie worked on a pro bono basis for years, providing detailed reports to the Board about his activities. [9] He was later appointed Vice President of the Board, which no doubt gave him some status on the Washington scene. Eventually, Board members Allen Sapp, Lester Glick, and Steven Jay successfully arranged for a special NEA grant to support his position for six months,[10] and he was given the title of Special Consultant, Governmental Relations and Development.

Ernie was adept at networking. Both he and Marcy took to the advocacy effort like ducks to water. By January 1980, the Guild had successfully developed working relationships with several key national music and arts education associations in Washington,[11] various officials at the NEA and other important policy-making bodies including the U.S. Department of Education, the Federal Council on the Arts and Humanities, the National Arts Awards, Educational Testing Service and others. In due course, the Guild also became a member of several key committees and task forces.[12] Most importantly, it was given a leading role in the Assembly of National Arts Education Organizations (ANAEO), a coalition which was set up to "manufacture and monitor legislation affecting arts education." [13]

The Guild had begun to gain a much-needed level of visibility among decision makers at the federal level. If the goal was to build awareness over time, these classic advocacy strategies were pertinent and productive. The Guild was educating the power brokers and building support for constituent schools. But if the goal was also to secure grants for the Guild itself from these sources, there was only a slim chance the effort would succeed in the short term. Besides, it was still too small to carry any clout in the Washington arts education lobbies with a cast of thousands. To wield meaningful influence in this thicket of conflicting interests would have needed a much greater long-term investment of dollars and personnel than the Guild possessed. In fact, at one point, Lester Glick was moved to create the phrase "imperial bureaucracy" to describe the maze of Washington offices, bureaus, and departments which needed to be navigated.

In a commentary attached to one of his reports, Ernie pointed out that the programs offered by Guild schools were in the vanguard of federal efforts to support arts education. But then, as now, "arts education" meant different things to different groups. In an attempt to find consensus, ANEAO was even considering the establishment of a National Institute for Arts Education, "if only to find a small group of individuals in Washington who [could] understand the term: arts education." [14]

It is doubtful that "arts education" could have been defined broadly enough to satisfy all of the players in the arts education coalitions. It is essentially a term which can be adapted to a host of educational activities with the arts at their center (or at the fringe). Advocacy is, after all, the art of self-interest and the eclectic nature of arts education lends itself to any number of interpretations and justifications, as was shown by the intense debates over the "extrinsic" and "intrinsic" purposes of the arts several decades later.

Two years after Marcy's appointment, Lester Glick was again able to give an upbeat report on the state of the Guild at the Toronto Conference, which must surely have heartened all present. He began by praising the Executive Director: "Marcy Horwitz has performed preeminently and grows in stature as the Guild grows. The same can be said for her administrative aide, Sandie Kaplan." [15]

Best of all, he went on to report that the Board was no longer made up primarily of school directors and that there were "just about" an equal number of school directors and lay members. "We have a distinguished Board," he said, "one that includes several of the top arts educators in the United States and experts in other fields such as arts management, media and higher education." To cap it all, he cited the Treasurer's Report, which stated that the Guild had been operating in the black all year and that it was "living within the budget." [16] His report omitted one other promising, first-time development: the door to a private foundation had been opened by Lester himself as a lay Board member, resulting in a grant for the Internship Program from the George Gund Foundation. It was an important model for the Board to emulate.

Characteristically, Lester underplayed his own role in bringing about these changes. "I took my direction from Lester," said Marcy. "He was my mentor. If it made [him] happy it was the right thing to do. He was driving the organization, not so much in terms of the decisions, but in terms of direction." [17] That level of trust was mutual.

Meanwhile, the Guild's Chapters were beginning to take root and regional programs were being developed independent of the national conferences. The chapter structure enabled the schools to create their own regional programs, adding another level of value to their membership in the Guild. For example, the New York Chapter initiated an annual joint recital at Alice Tully Hall, featuring students from schools in the Chapter. As a public relations effort this was highly effective since they were able to attract top level artists who were alumni of Guild schools such as Sidney Harth, Jose Feliciano, and Garrick Ohlsson to perform as well. Ads were placed in *The New York Times* and paid for by contributions from each school. In time, the Guild was able to get funding from the New York State Council for the Arts for chapter activities in New York.

The Guild was more or less reinventing itself as it went along with creative iterations of programs and services within Marcy's overall rubric of Education, Communication, Research, and Advocacy. One service of particular value to the membership was the publication of survey results relating to administrative expenses such as staff and faculty salaries, benefits, administrative costs, and so on. Also, member schools were learning to computerize their payroll and office procedures through the pioneering efforts of Guild Trustee, Kal Novak, Executive Director of the Music Center of the North Shore, Winnetka, IL, who offered both conference workshops and technical assistance.

In early 1979, Marcy learned with some regret that the ACA's lease had been terminated. Their location near Carnegie Hall had been ideal. However, there was nothing to be done but to move yet again, this time to the landmark Flatiron Building at 175 Fifth Avenue in New York.

By June of that year, midway into Marcy's tenure, the Guild had settled into a comfortable, conflict-free mode of operation. In terms of governance, the Board had successfully recruited enough lay members so they now represented about half the number of trustees[18] and a rotation policy was in the works. It had also taken the unprecedented step of requiring all Board members to sign on as dues-paying individual members. However, revenues from those dues did not directly benefit the Guild. Instead they were allocated to "travel expenses for our West Coast/California Trustees."[19] The number of institutional members had grown to 65 and the budget was a manageable $61,000. The office was running smoothly, the membership felt reasonably contented (in spite of a dues increase), annual grants of $20,000 each from the NEA and the Music Performance Trust Funds were, to all intents and purposes, assured, and programs and services to the field were satisfactory.

Curiously, little attention was given to fundraising for programs and services through foundation or individual contributions – a standard strategy for most non-profits. The Board could not be counted on to fill that gap from its own personal resources since the Trustees were no wealthier in the aggregate than before the recruitment of lay members. Neither were the Trustees able (or willing) to introduce the Guild to potential grant makers.

The Board had not specifically tasked the Executive Director with responsibility for raising funds. When asked years later whether she had any desire to do so, Marcy responded that she didn't have any fundraising experience at that point in her life. "I don't think I understood what we could have done if we had aggressively pursued funds." [20]

Marcy's lack of experience or interest in this regard raised no red flags with the Board or membership. Things were going along pretty smoothly. Why rock the boat when Marcy was the one who had righted it? A skilled mentor could have helped. But none was forthcoming. By and large, the fundraising issue was simply swept under the rug ostensibly because of the fear of competition with member schools.

Inevitably, financial stresses began to surface. For eighteen months starting in early 1980, the Guild was in a state of suspended animation. To all outward appearances, it was functioning smoothly and planning with good faith for the future. But internally, daily activities were infused with anxiety, a sense that the axe might fall at any time.

Even at this distance of time, the downward spiral in resources and personnel makes for distressing reading. The chronology speaks for itself.

January 18, 1980: Responding to "the current cash-flow crisis," Allen Sapp, recently elected Board President, arranges for a modest, interest-free bridge loan from the New York Foundation for the Arts. He also donates his travel allowance back to the Guild.

April 9, 1980: Cash flow problems recur. Pay checks are withheld. Rent and telephone bills are unpaid. [21]

April 25, 1980: The Finance Committee notes its dissatisfaction with the current cash-flow problem, and the measures taken to deal with [it]. Staff is asked by the Executive Committee to "exercise all possible restraint...and to make every effort to recoup all outstanding income."

April 25, 1980: Ernie reports on his meeting with Allen Sapp to discuss "the progress and future of the National Guild." They offer three suggestions to ensure internal stability: 1) Develop a fund-raising plan, 2) Increase efforts to recruit new member schools, and 3) Invest dollars and personnel to publicize the Guild's activities. No action follows.

May 15, 1980: The $6,000 grant from the NEA to support the Washington Office expires. Ernie's position is terminated.

June 2, 1980: Marcy reminds the Board that the NEA grant of $15,000 for the period 1980 through February 28, 1981 will not be renewed by the Music Program. The Guild is directed to approach NEA's new Inter-Arts Program where its multi-arts profile is considered a better fit.

June 2, 1980: After a call to Inter-Arts, Marcy writes an urgent letter to the Finance Committee advising members that because of differences in deadlines, there will be a four-month fallow period during which there will be "absolutely no NEA money at our disposal." The subject heading is "MAYDAY." She appeals for constructive solutions.

June 27, 1980: Marcy expresses increasing anxiety about operational procedures, namely, that some committees are not pulling their weight. Twelve Trustees attend the Board meeting that day. There are twenty-seven no-shows.

June 27, 1980: Sandra attaches an italicized note about the shortfall to her financial report to the Board: *These monies must be secured by*

January 1981 in order to enable the continuation of the National Guild as we now know it.

June 27, 1980: The Board makes minor amendments to the budget at its meeting. There is no change in the $60,000 bottom line. Following the mindset of years, the Guild assumes that at least some portion of the Inter-Arts grant will be forthcoming, and an estimated $15,000 shows up under the Income column presumably as a fund-raising goal. Regardless, the budget still projects a shortfall of $8,000, the amount needed to operate the national office during the fallow period.

July 22, 1980. The duration of the "fallow period" is amended from four to seven months. [22]

November 10, 1980: The Board requests the Finance, Executive, and Long Range Planning Committees to work on a "fallback position [in case] a real crisis arises and we are not funded by the Inter/Arts Program." Member schools are encouraged to write to Livingston Biddle, NEA's Chairman, urging support for the Guild.

November 11, 1980: The Executive Committee accepts responsibility for raising $8,000.

A decision is taken to avoid presenting the shortfall to the membership as a crisis "but as a short-term problem that…could be resolved with a loan."

November 11, 1980: The Finance Committee refers the Board to a policy statement issued by the NEA, which states bluntly that NEA will support no organization forever, in the belief that an organization must come to a point where it is self-supporting.

January 30, 1981: Marcy Horwitz resigns with effect from May 15, 1981 (later extended to end-May). She stresses that her resignation is not "triggered by any event or combination of events; rather, after nearly five years I felt the need for a change." "I felt very much out of touch with real schools," she wrote later.[23] Shortly afterwards, she is appointed Director of Concerts at Third Street Music School in New York.

May 27, 1981: The Guild is informed that the grant application to NEA's Inter-Arts program has been turned down. The decision leaves a gaping hole of $15,000 in the FY 81-82 budget. The decision is final. Sandra is told that "the Guild's small membership base and lack of corporate funding" weighed against approval. The $8,000 shortfall plus the $15,000 denial leaves the Guild with a total deficit of $23,000 – nearly 40% of the budget.

May 29, 1981: With just 17 out of 42 Trustees present at its meeting, the Board goes into a full crisis mode, opening up a free-ranging discussion of both immediate and long-range remedies including finding a temporary home at a member school or hiring interns. Allen Sapp reports on his meeting with Joan Armstrong at Inter-Arts. She tells him there was concern about the size of the grant requested ($25,000). Alvin (Skip) Reiss offers to check with the NEA about the availability of dollars for development of corporate support. Monroe Levin feels that the Guild's membership needs to be expanded. There is $1,603 in the bank. Payables are just under $6,000. Modest receivables are trickling in. A bare bones budget of $41,000 for 1981-82 is approved.

May 29, 1981: David Greer reminds the Board that the Guild will be without an executive director "at 5:00 p.m. tonight." Sandra points out that there will be nobody in the office to open the mail after July 3, her last day at the Guild.

May 29, 1981: Board President Allen Sapp describes at length the situation in his professional life that has created unforeseen personal pressures. He seeks additional help in carrying out his leadership responsibility in the coming months.

May 29, 1981: At the end of the meeting, the Board expresses its thanks to Marcy and Sandra. They are informed that gifts would soon be forthcoming which should be taken as "an earnest token of our feeling, our love and our appreciation."

That recognition was well deserved. The two young women had taken over an organization in great turmoil and brought it to a place of calmness and order. Marcy is affectionately remembered by her contemporaries for holding the Guild together with cheery efficiency at a perilous time. More importantly, she was successful in bringing the Guild to the notice of power brokers in Washington, and it was being included in a growing number of major policy making forums and studies, including David Rockefeller's seminal "Coming to Our Senses" report in the late seventies. She can be rightly proud of those achievements. But lacking a background in finance or development, she was unable to anticipate (or avert) the consequences of chronically shaky finances. Neither was she inclined to challenge the Guild's comfort level in the midst of good times. In terms of her legacy, it could be said with truth that she left behind her an organization high on morale but low on resources.

Chapter Six
The New Hire

Once more into the breach, dear friends, once more.

– William Shakespeare[1]

T he Guild was now without an executive director, without a functioning board president, and without the means to survive.

Into this vacuum stepped Henry Bridges, the founder and director of Charlotte's Community Music School in North Carolina. Henry was the Guild's Vice President, having served as a Board member since 1975. With his laid-back, courteous manner, and gentle sense of humor he could easily be taken for a classic Southern Gentleman. But behind that graceful façade there lived a determined and natural-born leader. Without fuss or fanfare, he just took charge. Never has a "coup" such as this been greeted with greater relief. This much is certain: were it not for Henry, the Guild would surely have folded.

Henry's first challenge was to hire an executive director, a task of no mean proportions given the meager annual salary of $16,000 on offer. Nine candidates had already submitted resumes and five were short-listed. It is not clear from the records if salary levels were disclosed.

Initially, the Board had hoped to find a temporary home for the Guild at a member school. Asked if he might be able to provide rent-free space at the Third Street Music School, its Executive Director, Robert Christensen generously agreed to help out – with a caveat. "The Guild is in an extremely precarious financial and organizational state and I would not like our School to be [its] burial ground." He added with some vehemence: "It is unconscionable to me that a full-time Executive Director and a part-time Executive Secretary are being sought." As an alternative, he proposed that a full-time Executive Secretary be hired and offered himself temporarily as an unpaid Executive Director.[2]

On the second Monday following Bob's letter, the Search Committee reported to the "Executive Board" that four people had been interviewed for the job of Executive Director out of a field of nine applicants. [3] The Committee was chaired by James Abruzzo, a professional search consultant who had donated his services. One candidate was recommended for the position. Nevertheless, exercising due diligence, the Board decided to interview all four finalists either in person or by phone. At the conclusion of that process, a motion was made to "engage Lolita Mayadas as Executive Director of the National Guild of Community Schools of the Arts." The motion passed unanimously.

To resolve the pending issue about the Presidency, Henry wrote a note to Allen Sapp: "In response to your telegram of June 26, 1981, I have acted with full powers of the President with respect to the search process. With the employment of Lolita Mayadas the search process has been completed." He added, "With your permission, I shall continue to act with the full powers of the President until such time as my services in this capacity are no longer needed."[4] Henry was now *de facto* President but Allen was still the *de jure* head of the Board. On August 3, 1981, a letter to the membership was issued over Allen's name.

It is with great enthusiasm that I introduce to you Lolita Mayadas, the new Executive Director of our National Guild. Mrs. Mayadas is a graduate of Queens College [School] and the Royal College of Music in London, England. She is an experienced pianist and teacher and has an extensive background in [music] education and arts administration: for ten years she was Executive Director of the Calcutta School of Music in India, for three years she was Registrar and Dean of Students of the Hochstein

School of Music in Rochester, New York, and for one year each she was Director of Administration for the Florida Philharmonic in Miami and the Grove Dance Theater, Miami.

Mrs. Mayadas was interviewed by our Search Committee, chaired by James Abruzzo, and by our Executive Committee. Both Committees were unanimously enthusiastic in recommending the employment of Lolita Mayadas.

There is a story behind these bare facts.

Around the middle of May 1981, I was preparing to make my way from Miami to the New York area with my husband Azim and our youngest daughter, Priya, leaving our older girls, Ayesha and Tanya at their respective colleges. Scouting around for a part-time job, I called Helen Tuntland (now Helen Jackson) who told me the Guild was in the final stages of selecting an Executive Director. One thing led to another. The next call was to Marcy, then James Abruzzo, and lastly, Henry Bridges. All four encouraged me to throw my hat in the ring.

After that, things moved rather fast. James called and told me that I was scheduled for an interview in New York. He also said the Guild would most likely be housed at the Third Street Music School in lower Manhattan. I thought a trial commute might be a good idea. The round trip from my home in Teaneck, New Jersey took more than 2 hours. I was not prepared to do that every day. So, I called James and said I was sorry but I was not interested. He demurred. "It's too late to cancel," he said. "Why don't you just show up for the interview and go from there?" I agreed. I didn't think the logistics of the job would work for me, but I was fascinated by the Guild. I knew what it represented and I shared its goals. Most importantly, I knew it from the grassroots, having worked at Hochstein for three years with Helen Tuntland, its Director, and my friend, mentor, and unofficial guru. It would not be an exaggeration to say Hochstein was the model and ideal training ground for my subsequent job with the Guild. I loved everything about my work there – the people, the camaraderie, the sense of compassionate humanity, and its overarching service mission.

It was a salutary education for someone who had been brought up in the conservatory tradition. Anyhow, before showing up for my interview, I did my homework based on my experiences at Hochstein, making voluminous notes on what I felt the Guild could be doing for the field.

I remember that blistering July afternoon as if it were yesterday. The Board meeting was being held in borrowed space in the "prow" of the Flatiron Building in New York. There were perhaps a dozen people around the table. Henry greeted me and introduced everyone one at a time. Then, with a wicked little gleam in his eye he turned to me and said, "Now tell us who we all are!" Even in jest, this was one of those sink or swim moments. I launched into a recitation of names:

Michael Pollon, Hadassah Markson, Annetta Kaplan, David Greer, George Bennette, Monroe Levin and so on until I got to one person near the end whom I couldn't place. I grinned, threw up my hands and said, "Oh forget it!" Everyone laughed. In the most serendipitous of ways the incident had broken the ice. Curiously, it was remembered by many of those present long after the substance of the meeting was forgotten. I told Henry years later that the joke was on him because I was familiar with all these names from my time at Hochstein. All I had to do was to put a face to each one. [5]

We got down to more serious issues. I was asked about my thoughts concerning the Guild. What were my ideas? What did I think I could bring to the job? Did I have any questions? I had done my homework and I shared my notes in detail: more members, better P.R. and communications, increased services, improved publications and above all, intensive fundraising. A lengthy and stimulating discussion followed. In terms of my experience, the Board seemed pleased that I was familiar with MPTF, a complex revenue-sharing program which I had administered at the Hochstein Music School. I was also a trained touch typist and office manager and I could, therefore, dispense with the services of a secretary.

In spite of all the positive aspects of the job, I informed the Board with regret that I could not accept it, if offered. My reasons were first, the lengthy commute and second, the $16,000 annual compensation. I told them I wasn't prepared to spoil my "marketability" by taking on a full-time position at that salary. However, I made an offer: on paper, make this a part-time position. If hired, I assured them, I would put in a full day's work. Privately, I thought they would surely consider this to be a preposterous and unacceptable suggestion and reject it.

They asked me to leave the room and went into a huddle.

When I returned, they asked if the office could be moved into my house in Teaneck, New Jersey. Though surprised, I agreed immediately – it seemed like the ideal solution. The Guild would save the rent and I would save the time and energy for the commute. They also agreed to hire me (on paper) for an average of 25 hours per week[6] on the tacit understanding that I would work full time. A vote was taken and the deal was closed. There was general satisfaction and relief all round, but also some skepticism. The Guild had just hired its fourth executive director in the space of eight years. Would this one work out? No doubt all the Board members had their fingers firmly crossed.

Many years later, I asked a couple of Board members why I got the job aside from my resume. Henry's response was, "Well, first I think is… enormous charm and diplomacy which was very obvious in that first interview. The National Guild was just a shred. There wasn't much left of the National Guild. And of course, we were desperate. [It was] then or never on that day. I think I felt, and I think all of us felt at the very beginning that we had unbelievable good fortune in this charming person that came to interview." [7] "I was so impressed with you. I remember I was very taken with you," said Hadassah Markson. "You were very articulate and a very 'up' kind of person. You'd be a leader. Maybe you could take this organization and turn it around." [8]

Although not known for her sense of humor, Annetta Kaplan had the last word. "You got the job because of your accent." [9]

There was no time to lose. The Flatiron lease was due to expire at the end of July. Azim and I rolled up our sleeves, packed up everything in the New York office, and arranged for a mover to ship it all to our home at 665 Northumberland Avenue in Teaneck, New Jersey. And there, in our spacious basement, we set up shop with two wooden desks, several meticulously organized file cabinets, the mimeograph machine, two IBM Selectric typewriters, a hefty Gestetner copier, and a large rubber apron covered with ink stains.

What hit me immediately was the loneliness of the job. No one visited. Barely anyone called. One of the first things I did was to reach out to all the Board members (Trustees) who were not present at the interview to introduce myself and to pick their brains. Those calls were cordially welcomed by these seasoned leaders, many of whom were considered to be giant figures in the Guild. For my part, the insight and suggestions I received from them were invaluable as a sort of orientation and sounding board. Soon, my calls to school directors and trustees from that distant basement became standard procedure. They were as much a way to combat my isolation as to get feedback and support for new ideas.

Two floors up, Azim was becoming more and more intrigued by the mission and history of the Guild and began researching its roots in the settlement house movement. On his own initiative, he also drew up maps showing the concentration of Guild member schools in the populated East coast, West coast, and Midwest regions. It was from him that I learned about the "empty quarter" from the Midwest to California and the vast areas of the South that were only sparsely populated with community schools.

I set to work preparing a draft budget together with a detailed set of proposals (based on the notes I had prepared for my interview) and presented them to the Long-Range Planning Committee chaired by Henry. These proposals laid out my vision and goals for the Guild for years to come. [10] The accompanying memo is excerpted below:

> It is my considered view that the general direction and development of the National Guild administration over the next few years should be guided by a development plan designed to increase the strength, visibility, and presence of this long-established institution. The aim of such a plan is not just survival but a building process.
>
> I am taking the liberty of making specific proposals for your consideration. These ...could be implemented over a period of time [through] a planned pattern of growth

depending upon the generation, and thus the availability, of funds. Clearly, the support the Guild receives is in direct proportion to the services it provides. It is my intention therefore to gradually expand appropriate services to the membership within a framework of fiscal responsibility.

As to the philosophy behind these proposals, the emphasis will be on the Guild, not as an independent, single unit but on the Guild as [the] representative of the schools and their interests.

In terms of the current year's budget, the memo noted: The Guild this year [will save] a substantial amount in rent, salaries, and related costs. The net amount of $18,980 [in savings] more than compensates for the loss of the expected NEA grant of $15,000.

These documents were presented to a new ad-hoc New York Liaison Committee at a meeting in late July at the Bloomingdale House of Music attended by Henry, David Greer, Director of Bloomingdale House of Music, and Michael Pollon, Director of the Westchester Conservatory of Music. We had an exhaustive and productive discussion of the proposals I had put forward. Then David spoke up. "If you think you can do all that," he said firmly, "you're all wet." After I had gotten to know him, I realized that David always said exactly what was on his mind, without equivocation. In time, I came to value his candor and honesty and we became very good friends. I also discovered that he was a worry wart without equal.

But at this point, David's remark was more than Michael Pollon could take. His chivalrous nature and Austrian upbringing simply could not countenance such behavior. He was horrified. He asked me not to take David's comments personally. We walked down the stairs together and out onto the little stoop. He put his hand gently on my arm. "Just take the ball and run with it," he said. And that's just what I did.

Chapter Seven
The Path Forward

The question is not when we came here...but...what we did after we arrived.

— Jimmy Carter[1]

Early one morning, I received a call from Michael Garroway, who was, at the time, the Chair of the New England (or Northeast) Chapter. "What are you going to do about the Guild?" he demanded, adding that if something were not done soon he would take steps to pull all his Chapter schools out of the Guild. I had been in place for just three weeks. I could say little in response. He seemed to be airing a grievance rather than seeking an answer. I do not recall whether he was speaking for himself or for the Chapter as a whole. This was not the first time a regional chapter had threatened to pull out from the Guild *en masse*. But for me, it was an early indication of the monumental task before us.

Three months into my tenure, a newly resurgent Allen Sapp wrote me a letter: [2] Allen was, at the time, Dean of the College-Conservatory of Music, University of Cincinnati, Ohio.

"I know that you must be feeling proud of managing so well your first Guild conference [in Cincinnati]. It was done splendidly with the easy grace of a professional and the constant hand of a dedicated administrator....I got a sense that the old hands are steady, ready for you to take a strong stance on matters. I urge you to be as aggressive as you have been, always cautioning that the one area not to neglect is formal and frequent communication with your officers. You can do almost anything if you communicate your intentions and plans reasonably....I urge you to make the expansion of the Guild into the South the main focus of your activity aside from the fund-raising which you can well handle in New York."

A graduate of Harvard University, Allen was a highly respected academic and composer and one of the most humane intellectuals I know. I came to admire his ability to define the issues at hand and his visceral understanding of what the Guild stood for. He was a candid, articulate, sometimes trenchant writer, and I always learned something from what he wrote. I was fortunate to have him as a guide, philosopher, and friend.

On October 15, 1981, the Board approved the implementation of my long-range proposals as a "blue-print for a phased pattern of growth" with every member voting in favor, including David Greer, our anxious resident skeptic.[3] A budget of $42,000 for the current year was also unanimously approved. In our shared enthusiasm, we adopted a set of budget projections (see below) that were highly optimistic, to say the least.

Projections (Summary)*

Year	Institutional Members	Contributed Income	Earned Revenue	Budget Total Income
1981-82 (Current)	68	0	42,000	$42,000
1982-83	83	24,425	45,575	$70,000
1983-84	98	34,800	49,200	$84,000
1984-85	113	45,175	53,825	$99,000
1985-86	128	51,810	65,690	$117,500

*Edited November 2017 for purposes of clarification.

With the proposed addition of just one administrative assistant, we anticipated both a doubling of the institutional membership and a major increase in contributed income within five years. Given the Guild's spotty record in these areas, these goals represented a nearly impossible vision. Was this a fool's paradise? Maybe. But few of us admitted to such thoughts at the time. It is astonishing how contagious and energizing a "can-do" attitude can be. And enthusiasm and passion can achieve many things that, on paper, seem completely undoable. Besides, new hires are usually given extensive latitude, and the Guild's Board is to be applauded for the confidence they placed in me as their new Executive Director, especially since the "blue-print" I proposed was driven by gut instinct rather than rational analysis.

There were two key differences in my approach to what had gone before. The first was to capitalize on the goodwill of the Board and membership with a plan that was bold and forward- thinking. And second was my view that the Guild should function as the representative of the <u>entire</u> field of community arts schools, not just its members. Prior to 1982, the Guild's services to the field had been defined for all practical purposes as services to members only. In other words, the benefits conferred on member schools in return for their membership fees were unavailable to non-members. I believed that this approach was parochial and self-defeating and began to offer benefits to our broader constituency of non-members on an *a la carte* basis at higher pro-rated prices. This approach was not universally supported, but I felt it had practical value and adopted it without a big song and dance as long as the Board and membership tacitly accepted it.

For logistical and other reasons, Board meetings were held just three times each year. Even with the best of intentions, regular communication with a large group of 40 trustees was necessarily limited. So, I started the tradition of making a written progress report to the Board at every meeting. The first report on February 5, 1982 (summarized below) shows extensive activity for the first six months of my tenure.

Administration and Governance

- Office relocated to Teaneck, New Jersey. All legal requirements completed.

- Audit for 1980-81 completed.

- Improved cash flow; $5,000 invested in Merrill Lynch Government Funds.

- Five-year development plan approved by the Board as a "blue-print."

- Advisory Council established under the Chairmanship of Lester Glick.

- Regular written reports from the E.D. distributed to the Board prior to every meeting.

Services to the Field

- National conference held in Cincinnati from October 15-18, 1981 jointly with the College Music Society (CMS). Attended by 55 delegates from the Guild and approximately 150 from CMS.

- Detailed questionnaire in two parts mailed to all institutional members prior to the publication of an annual report on school statistics.

- Bi-monthly Guildletter increased in size, scope, and distribution. Mailing list expanded from 300 to 1500 individuals and organizations.

- Monthly notice of Employment Opportunities introduced.

- All-day Regional Workshop on Planning and Setting Goals presented by John Urice for the New York Chapter. 17 participants attended.

- Monthly Guild mailgrams for institutional members introduced.

Membership

- 57 letters sent out to all Preparatory Divisions of Colleges and Conservatories which had attended a special conference in Rochester, New York, under the behest of Vincent Lenti, Director of the Eastman School of Music Community Education Division.

- Shorter and "more effective" membership application designed.

- Three new member schools recruited.

P.R and Communications

- Guild Handbook for informational and promotional purposes prepared for distribution to potential members and grantmakers.

Fundraising and In-kind Contributions

- Grant application submitted to the National Endowment for the Arts (Expansion Arts – Services to the Field) for $5,000 to support the newsletter.

- Prudential Life agreed to print an indefinite number of newsletters for the Guild without charge, thanks to Susan Male and Benjamin Dunham. [4]

- C. W. Shaver and Company agreed to provide the following pro bono services to the Guild. 1) A regular article entitled "Money Talk" for Guildletter covering new developments in fundraising; new tax laws regarding donations; the latest news about Federal funding to the arts, humanities, and social services; fund-raising techniques; possible new sources of funding; foundation news, etc. 2) A Staff Consultant to serve on the Guild's Fundraising Committee. 3) Shaver will also consider updating their 1973 Manual on Fundraising for Community Music Schools.

By November 1981, the Guild's office was in full swing, with me as head cook and bottle-washer. Even though I had been hired officially on a part-time salary, I had assured the Board during my initial interview with them that I would be willing to work full-time. But now, through sheer necessity, I found myself putting in long hours well into the evenings and weekends.

To express their appreciation, the Board increased my salary on February 5 to $17,500 retroactively from January 1, 1982. The extra cash was more than welcome, but as time went on my appreciation was mixed with a sinking feeling that I would need to raise it myself.

Ungracious? Undoubtedly. But it would be more than two decades before the Guild had a functioning Fund Raising Committee and a Board with the personal resources and potential donor connections to back up their fundraising goals.

I have some nostalgic memories of how we prepared memos in bulk in those days. We had never heard of a computer except in the same way we now think of robots – fascinating, but way beyond our reach. Everything had to be done by hand, exactly in order. To start, you rolled a special sheet of stencil paper into the typewriter and typed out your memo. If you made a mistake you took a little brush and applied what looked like colorless nail polish to the offending spot. You waited five minutes for it to dry, completed your typing, pulled the stencil out and then walked it over to your mimeograph machine. You donned your rubber apron and inked the rollers. Then, after much trial and error you got the ink to spread evenly at which point you placed your stencil on the roller and cranked the handle. Voila! Of course, if you wanted something fancy with typeface then you had to run out and buy a Letraset sheet. Then you laboriously pressed each letter out on the paper by hand. It was great fun! Except that it took half a day just to prepare the cover for, say, a conference program or other publication. And finally, there was the cumbersome mailing and labeling process. Many's the time I corralled visitors to our home to participate in "mailing parties" and almost unfailingly they took on their labors with energy and good humor.

In June 1982, a detailed 3-year budget was presented to Richard (Dick) Letts, Chairman of the Goals and Planning Committee. [5] Concurrently, Henry Bridges asked Dick to begin a review of the Guild's goals and objectives. Little did I realize that this innocuous request would become the catalyst for an impassioned exchange of correspondence between Dick, members of the Planning Committee, and myself. The exchange, reproduced in full below, is worth reading if only as a reflection of disparate points of view prevailing at the time.

6/18/82 Richard Letts to Henry Bridges (on the eve of Dick's departure for Australia where he had been appointed Director of the Music Board of the Australia Council.)

As Planning Chair of the Guild, I was asked by you to begin a review of the Guild's goals and objectives. Only a small beginning has been made. Given the need to use such a review as a means of involving the members more in the Guild, I think it would be counter-productive for the process to continue under a Chair who will not see it through. So I pass the ball back to you, along…with a few parting thoughts.

Lolita has questioned the need for such a review at this time. As she is the person who will drive the Guild forward, I think we must take into consideration her reservations, especially if she feels that a review would get in the way of progress rather than stimulate it. However, I do have some thoughts on why the review might be needed, and offer these for your consideration.

I have some personal opinions and impressions (which may or may not be off-base) relating to the issue. During my association with the Guild it has had a fragile existence… Because the membership is supposed to serve greatly differing communities, criteria for membership has been kept to a minimum. Could it be true also that a

61

former commitment to socially conscious programs has been watered down in some schools, and no one quite wants to look at this? Anyway, it seems to me that all of this adds up to a situation in which it is not too clear what the Guild stands for, or how it defines itself.

There are some criteria for membership which we seem to take with seriousness...[such as non-profit status, evidence of fiscal responsibility, some sort of scholarship program and a commitment to quality.]

Of course, we do care, all of us about attaining the best possible quality programs. But who doesn't? Although this will always be a primary concern, it is hardly something which distinguishes Guild schools and the Guild from outsiders. Looking at the bigger world of music schools, we are pretty close to bottom of the pecking order in the quality issue. The musical world is not going to light up if we proclaim that this is what we stand for. We have been outflanked on the right.

Without knowing this from experience, I imagine that once the Guild stood very strongly for socially aware arts programming. The settlement school background. I hear less and less about this type of issue at Guild meetings. In the last few months, I have been very surprised to discover that there is a large body of theory and practice in community arts, with activities all over the world (including in the U.S.A.). I have never heard mention of this through the Guild. The Guild has been outflanked on the left, also.

We seem to be left in an amorphous middle ground, with no clear definitions or rallying points other than a somewhat watery commitment to 'scholarships' (collectively at least) and a mom and apple pie agreement about quality...

Perhaps the Guild doesn't have to stand for anything. Perhaps it could be just a service organization for any school that wants to join... In my opinion, the Guild would benefit by reasserting some strong beliefs about community arts, and by providing stimulation and mutual reinforcement for members who take the arts to places they otherwise would not go, preferably with flair, imagination, and quality.

There are times in the life of any service organization when a reassessment of mission and purposes is essential. To my mind this was not one of them. Soul searching can only too easily become an end in itself. I believed we urgently needed *actionable* goals and objectives to revive an organization already on life-support. To my mind, such an exercise in navel-gazing especially at this time was a distraction we could ill afford.

6/21/1982 Dick Kauffman to Richard Letts

The Guild has taken on a different dimension since I was on the old Goals and Planning Committee... with new standing committees: fund raising and P.R. (much of this was in the original Goals/Planning Committee's working plan), I feel we do need to take a new look as to what this committee is to do – and how it is to function. The budget committee, too, has taken on "a new look."

Member Schools and Individual Members will definitely feel more a part of the Guild if they become more involved. I believe that our goals must be to come up with a plan in which the Guild can and will be "important" for its members and to bring on new members. Attractive brochures – up to date, eye-catching, word-catching "info" – a solid financial base – think "international" (because of our Canadian friends) – more international programming of some sort using all forms of media possible – etc.

Seems to me that we need to meet in Charlotte and rap with one another about all of this, taking the reports of the various other committees and see how we can bring all of this together into a dynamic organization. Lolita should have a very important part in this too.

8/20/1982 Eileen T. Cline to Richard Letts

As I started this note to you, I checked a folder and realized that actually the Guild has already adopted its goals and objectives – though I seem to recall that some modifications have been made since last August. Perhaps what the planning committee could be especially helpful with is how the goals might be applied and implemented, both generally and in specific situations.

If you think that is an appropriate approach, it would help me considerably to have a working-paper from which to proceed. Perhaps you could ask Lolita to send each committee member an updated copy of the goals as they have been agreed upon, and we could go from there? If I were to get that around August 1 or so, I could get something concrete back to you before the end of August. Would appreciate your letting me know what you think of that approach, and will be happy to get right to it, if you think it a good one.

8/24/1982 Lolita Mayadas to Henry Bridges

I am afraid I do not concur with the idea of a review of the Guild's objectives based upon philosophical considerations. To my mind, the problems of the Guild are essentially practical ones which cannot be solved by a continual introspection about its "status." You will recall that there are several recommendations on file as to what the Guild should be doing to fulfill its purposes, from the Max Kaplan Report of 1966 to my own statement adopted by the Board last November. The real need is to get on and do what is required: widen the membership base; increase communications, visibility and public awareness; develop a consistent and reliable fund-raising capability; institute a viable advocacy role; and increase its services to the membership.

There is no argument about these goals and I do not feel that any doubts [about the Guild's purposes] would be resolved by a reference to the membership. On the contrary, this could be seen as a weakness in the leadership and lead to a lack of confidence, divisiveness and a certain *ennui* which could be extremely contagious. It would be preferable for the Committee to project a positive and dynamic role with a firm statement of goals and objectives.

As to the inclusion of prep schools in the Guild, let us not forget the near-panic there was last year when there was a real possibility of a parallel organization being formed at the Rochester, New York conference with Collegiate Prep Divisions in 1980-81. As you know, we have all agonized over this issue for some time and it is essential that we arrive at an acceptable solution. The Membership Committee is presently at work drafting a proposal for a category of membership which could include these schools in the Guild without undermining the philosophy of social/community service and which might even lead them to the path of "virtue." The proposal is to be voted on by the membership in September.

8/28/1982 Allen Sapp to Henry Bridges

My position (arrived at quite independently) is precisely that of Lolita's. I do not feel any philosophical review of Guild purposes is all that is needed or relevant. The fact is that there will always be at least four different important strands in the work of the Guild and that these strands will be manifest in various membership situations.

- The social service, community welfare strand identified strongly with the Settlement School Movement

- The Neighborhood Music Arts school providing reasonable instruction to the immediate neighborhood whether deep inner, urban or pastoral or suburban

- The Preparatory or Satellite Unit of a major University situation logistically supported by a broad-based parent and functioning within its philosophical and financial framework

- The more or less elaborate Independent School which is regionally rather than locally identified and constituted

Most people in the arts and education believe that there is a social value, spiritual value, service in building character through study of the arts. A few move into professional life but most remain connected to the Arts as a fortifying resource through life-expanding the connection or not as circumstances indicate. To keep trying to rationalize what is at the heart of every serious teacher of music, art, dance or crafts or visual arts is to belabor the obvious. In various ways and through various machineries we are all trying to bring literacy and illumination and insight into the sensory-rational equation which is what the arts are. The Guild folk know what they are about. They can be helped and guided by a National Organization which serves as a communications clearing house, an ardent representative in such policy-making forums as there (piffling few) are, an aggressive propagandist for the Community Arts, a purveyor of technical and consultative assistance to its constituents, and an embodiment in its leadership of the professional and moral factors which improve our missions. That is it.

What you should expect from the Long-Range Planning Committee – in my opinion – are ideas, specific items to be considered for emphasis at various times, and helpful assistance in establishing such goals through sensible staff work.

Anyhow – Do spare us from some windy, baggy, pompous, rhetorical, gaseous, dreary, pointless, and foolish dance around the icons of meaninglessness. Let Lolita alone and encourage her to do even more by: paying her a decent salary, giving her adequate travel funds, enlarging her staff, and expanding the technical equipment at her disposal. THAT IS LONG RANGE PLANNING reflecting common sense.

Lolita Mayadas

Chapter Eight
Candles in the Dark

We had no reason to be negative... You were sent from heaven.

– Kal Novak[1]

Planning was one thing. Implementation was something else entirely, especially given the frail state of the Guild. We were short of money, short of staff, short of a permanent home, and short of clout where it counted. Not to put too fine a point on it, the Guild had hit rock bottom. The situation was dire, but on the other hand...in the words of the old cliché, there was nowhere to go but up. Slowly, in small incremental steps, we began to make progress.

Within a year, things had settled down to the point where everyone seemed to be pulling together in the same general direction. There was a contagious sense of excitement and participation sustained by a credible promise of better times to come and, perhaps, relief that the new hire might turn out to be a wise choice after all.

That sentiment was expressed in a letter from Lester Glick to Henry on December 12, 1981, just four months after my appointment. "I have talked with Lolita several times since returning from London and each time [I] am impressed by her personality and her quick mastery of her job. She is a real pro."

I realized this was still the honeymoon period. Nevertheless, it was heartening to receive encomiums like this on both formal and informal occasions. I also welcomed what I took to be a validation of a leadership style that was intentionally assertive and direct. A "take-charge" approach seemed to be the only way to turn around an organization where decision-making was overly decentralized, where the governance/management structure was cumbersome (being modeled on a local rather than national organization), where so many questions surfaced so often as to who we are that we were rendered virtually impotent, and where risk-taking was…well, too risky. But it is also likely that those very characteristics that contributed to my success, and that of the Guild in those early years, also made me a lightning rod for naysayers down the line. Change brings about many unintended consequences. But all that was still in the distant future.

As of now, *esprit de corps* prevailed and no one was inclined to look a gift horse in the mouth.

Meantime, we were still critically short on resources and, inevitably, we encountered many dead ends. But significant progress was being made, if not uniformly, then at least in enough incremental ways that our spirits remained high and our resolve strong. We were functioning like entrepreneurs, building a new Guild on the foundation of the old. It was a truly exhilarating time, never to be repeated in quite the same way.

By the time the national conference in Charlotte, North Carolina, came around in November 1982, membership recruitment had picked up, and fundraising efforts were firmly on the front burner. We were happy to receive grants of $2,000 from the North Carolina State Arts Council for the Arts and $3,000 from the Mary Duke Biddle Foundation for support of the conference. Also, two proposals for $15,000 each had been submitted: the first to National Endowment for the Arts (Inter-Arts Program) to support expansion of services to the field and the second to the Knight Foundation for development support. Finally, an expanded list of 23 new foundation prospects was developed with names of Board members and other friends attached to each one.

Their job was to solicit potential sources, or to follow-up with proposals already submitted. The goal was to encourage Trustees to get involved in the fund-raising effort by assigning them specific, do-able tasks.

As for membership, we joyfully announced at the Charlotte conference that there were now 76 members – the largest in the

Guild's history up to that time – and that 36 other schools were being solicited for membership. As a result of that growth, there were now five regional chapters listed here together with their Chairs: NY Metropolitan – Hadassah Markson; New England – Jim Simpson; Eastern Great Lakes – Mary Leggatt; MidAtlantic – Robert Capanna; and West Coast – Stephen Shapiro.

There was good news all round. Henry Bridges confirmed at the November Annual Meeting that there was an 18% increase in membership and a 100% increase in conference registration over the previous year. Furthermore, he said that because of the "frugality" practiced by the Executive Director, the fund balance was a healthy $6,520, as compared to $1,814 the previous year.[2]

Also, a new category of Trustee membership was proposed whereby all Board members would be asked to contribute $75 annually to the Guild.

In terms of publications:

- A Membership Directory was published in July 1982 with expanded information on each member school.

- A new Member Profile Survey was issued containing detailed information on Faculty and Administrative Salaries and Tuition fee structures. The survey, by Alfred D. Andreychuck, was made possible through the support of the Center for Arts Administration, University of Wisconsin.

- The following newsletters were in the works: the Quarterly Guildletter, for general circulation, and the monthly Guildnotes for members only.

- A third newsletter called Guildpeople for a projected new category of faculty and student membership was also in the pipeline.

In our enthusiasm, we also came up with some wild ideas. Fortunately, they were soon discarded. The first to be abandoned was a proposal to open up a new category of student membership in the Guild. Member schools would be asked to subscribe to the quarterly

Guildpeople at the rate of $1 per student (in lieu of membership dues), and copies would be sent out in bulk to each school. The next was a proposal to issue a National Directory of Community Arts Organizations, soon rejected for reasons of cost and feasibility, and the third was a proposal to get 20 people to participate in a Russian Arts Adventure, organized by the Citizens Exchange Council. The program would have generated $100 per participant for the Guild for a net total of $2,000. But only one person signed up and the project was summarily dropped.

To state the obvious, there was enough going on, even without the addition of any new programs. I desperately needed more staff to deal with the growing daily workload, but our down-to-the-bone budget would not permit it. Our only hope was to turn to the NEA and pray that they would once again come to our aid. So we went ahead and made the application to the Inter-Arts Program for $15,000.

Several months later I received a call from Jonathan Katz, who had been assigned to visit the Guild by the NEA as a part of the grant review process.

At the time, Jonathan was the Executive Director of the National Assembly of State Arts Agencies. A ubiquitous and influential figure, he was highly respected in his field, and well-liked besides. There was a lot hanging on his visit to the Guild. Aside from the actual cash requested, we needed the imprimatur of the NEA and the credibility that would come with a renewed grant.

I greeted Jonathan at our front door and led him through our little beehive of a house – into the foyer, across the living room, past the dining room, into the kitchen, and down the stairs into our modest, sepia-paneled, neon-lit basement. There wasn't much daylight down there, just three narrow windows beneath the ceiling with a dusty, ground-level view of the weeds in our front yard; an unimpressive spot, to say the least.

Jonathan's warm, empathetic personality and ready smile made me feel at ease right away. But his job was to assess our eligibility and readiness for a grant award and he did not pull his punches. He asked a lot of detailed questions and inspected a slew of materials, including our home-made brochures. He even asked me about the contents of our filing cabinets.

We must have made a positive impression because to our great relief and delight, we received a letter from the NEA early the following year, approving an $8,400 grant. As was normal practice, the grant needed to be matched 1:1.

It should be noted that Jonathan's guidance going forward was indispensable to the Guild throughout his association with the organization. In particular, his inside knowledge of how partnerships work at both state and federal levels was an invaluable factor in the design and implementation of the seminal Creative Communities Initiative in 2000.

At almost every meeting up to that point, Stephen Shiman, Chair of the Fundraising Committee, had insisted that I be given a staff assistant to help with fund raising. At the same time, the Board wanted me to get more clerical assistance so that I, personally, could focus more on fundraising. For me, both options had merit, but neither responded to my vision of where we were going; neither looked beyond the basic administrative function. I was inclined to step outside that box. I felt instinctively that the greater need was for 1) an experienced business manager, and 2) someone who could help recruit new member schools and develop services to the membership. But, to state the obvious, resources were limited, and there was no way we could afford to hire new personnel with higher order skills and experience. Or…could we?

I agonized over this problem for many days and sleepless nights, but without result. Sometimes, solutions are so obvious we are unable to see them. One day, in a Eureka moment, it occurred to me that my husband Azim would be ideal. He was in between jobs, stuck in a dead-end consultancy, and looking around for better opportunities. And aside from his considerable management experience in senior corporate positions, he had the added advantage of being a musician and an active concert pianist.

Most importantly, he was already "sold" on the Guild, doing research in his own time on its roots in the settlement house movement in London and the evolution of that movement in Europe and America. Along the way, he had also prepared myriad maps, charts, and statistics which proved to be invaluable down the line. In terms of the usually thorny issue of husband and wife working together, Azim and I had developed successful working partnerships at the Calcutta School of Music as well as the Florida Philharmonic. I sounded out Henry Bridges and a couple of other Board members about hiring Azim, and I was encouraged to pursue this proposal with the Board. Accordingly, Azim's resume was sent to the Executive Committee for initial consideration.

At the next Board meeting on Friday, June 10, 1983, the Executive Committee reported that Mr. Mayadas was "most qualified for the position" and enthusiastically endorsed his part-time employment as Director of Membership Services. While recognizing that the Executive Director is usually authorized to hire her own staff, the Board realized that their approval was being sought in this case because of the husband/wife relationship. After some discussion concerning workability of the arrangement, the Board affirmed the appointment at an executive session.

At the same meeting the Board was informed that Bob Christensen was being asked to work on a pro bono basis as a fundraiser for the Guild for three months. After that period, he would receive a small stipend of $4,500 for another three months. At the close of the meeting, "Steve Shiman thanked Lolita Mayadas for her inspired leadership of the Guild. The entire Board joined in his words of appreciation."

A week later, the following announcements were issued:

The National Guild is…pleased to announce that Robert C. Christensen has been engaged to assist the Executive Director in fund-raising and development. Mr. Christensen has had extensive experience in this field both as Director of Development at the Hartt College of Music, University of Hartford and later as Executive Director of the Third Street Music School, New York. As a practicing musician,

Christensen holds a master's degree from the Eastman School of Music at the University of Rochester.

The National Guild of Community Schools of the Arts is [also] pleased to announce that the Board of Trustees...approved the appointment of Azim L. Mayadas as Director of Membership Services, effective July 18, 1983. Azim Mayadas has had extensive administrative experience in senior corporate positions as well as in major arts organizations. He received his education in the U.K., at London University [City and Guilds College] and at the Royal Academy of Music and subsequently worked as General Manager and Chief Executive Officer at national industrial corporations in India, both in the public and private sectors. He was also active in the community as a Trustee on the Boards of the Calcutta School of Music, the Sir Edward Benthall Charitable Trust, the Calcutta Management Association and the Asiatic Society....In 1975, he was appointed Assistant General Manager of the Rochester Philharmonic Orchestra, New York, and subsequently General Manager of the Florida Philharmonic in Miami. Since 1981, he has been running his own consulting company.

Considered a musical prodigy as a child, Azim was also a composer and active concert artist who performed frequently as a soloist in recital and with orchestras. He also gave regular broadcasts as a speaker and pianist and competed with distinction in international competitions.

The decision to appoint Azim was expedient but it was also remarkably prescient. We had hired him as our Director of Membership Services, but that job was just one aspect of what we eventually received from him. Possessed of an outsize intellect, he was a true polymath with wide-ranging interests in history, music, visual arts, science, philosophy, and philology. His interest in world languages motivated him to spend fifteen years developing an international language called COSMAL because he felt Esperanto was too complicated and difficult to learn.

There was nothing superficial in his approach to his job or his hobbies. He was a scholar who wore his learning lightly, not a dilettante. And he brought all of his knowledge and skills to the service of the Guild. Everything I ever learned about the genesis and evolution of community music schools was through him. And notably, he, his maps, and charts taught us how to design and carry out successful membership campaigns, thereby increasing annual earned revenues significantly. His approach was always strategic and analytical rather than tactical. But his instinctive grasp of the larger picture did not in any way undermine his ability to carry out administrative tasks that required the greatest detail. I believe it is fair to say that his work laid the foundation upon which the Guild was able to construct all of its programs and to grow its resources. He was, quite simply, indispensable.

The results of Azim's efforts more than justified his hiring. Between July and November 1983, he had successfully persuaded 21 schools to apply for membership, and all except one had been evaluated by independent visitors to determine eligibility. 18 of these institutions were elected as members by the Board on November 13, 1983. Within two years, he had succeeded in doubling the membership to 150 schools. By 1988 there were 200 members, and by 1998 we had 250 member institutions — more than three times the number he had started with, even accounting for attrition. By the time he retired in 2001 (as Managing Director), the Guild's membership directory listed nearly 320 certified institutions.

It would not be an exaggeration to say that if there was one single factor that resulted in greater recognition and credibility for the Guild, it was the sustained pace of rapid growth in membership achieved in a relatively short period of time. The expansion was not just a matter of geography. It was also reflected in the profile of new member schools which embraced diversity of structure, of community, and of art forms.

Referring to Azim's hiring in a letter dated November 19, 1991 after the Annual Meeting that year (following the announcement of the Lila Wallace-Reader's Digest Fund grant), Guild Trustee Monroe Levin wrote to Lolita:

"Your tribute to Azim stressed the one thing without which all else would not have mattered – expansion of the membership. Pardon me, therefore, for accepting credit in the area of flaunting the rules against nepotism. When the usual objections to adding Azim and rehiring him came up, I said we were going to become the classic exception to the rule. Anyone seeing all those charts projected on the Clarion Hotel's huge screen would have to agree we were right."

It has to be remembered that the membership recruitment process at that time was not just a simple matter of seeking and accepting applications. Every school was required to go through a process of evaluation (including a site visit) and to demonstrate a commitment to quality and accessibility before it could join the Guild. Thus, every member institution met a set of basic standards while also sharing a cohesive mission with every other.

With membership growth gathering momentum in 1983, we turned our attention to fundraising. Here, we were fortunate to have the services of Bob Christensen. As Executive Director of the Third Street Music School, Bob had long experience with foundation and corporate giving in New York, and our hope was that his many contacts would turn out to be valuable to the Guild. One of his first suggestions was to contact the Exxon Corporation for an unrestricted gift.

For my part, I had no idea where to start – obviously, I couldn't just make a cold call and ask for general operating support. I needed someone to open that door. Bob thought Betty Allen could be helpful. Betty was a renowned American opera diva – and a part of the first generation of African American opera singers to achieve wide success. [3] In 1979 she was appointed Executive Director of the Harlem School of the Arts following the retirement of Dorothy Maynor, its founder. She was also one of the Guild's Honorary Trustees. She had a commanding presence, befitting her reputation and star power. I called her up.

Next thing I knew, she marched me up to the Exxon Corporation to meet with Leon Fleischer, who was the head of the arts giving program. "Leon," she said, "this is Lolita Mayadas. She needs some money." He asked me to elaborate. I did the best I could and promised a request in writing. Several weeks later, we got a letter approving an unrestricted grant of $1,500.

Then, one day that summer, I got a call from Ben Dunham, who was the Executive Director of Chamber Music America. He had been elected to the Guild's Board in October 1981. He was a consummate professional who was deeply committed to the mission of the Guild. "I've just been speaking to Dianne Daniels at the Charles Ulrick and Josephine Bay Foundation," he told me. "She would be willing to consider a proposal from the Guild for $10,000 to match the NEA grant. Why don't you get that in right away?" [4] I couldn't believe my ears! I thanked him profusely. But as soon as I put the phone down, I tossed decorum to the winds, jumping up and down like some 5-year-old kid. And indeed, in due course we had the grant in hand. This was also the beginning of a highly productive relationship with the Foundation, resulting in a major grant for the Guild's "Partners in Excellence" Program in 2000. PIE was a major national initiative, which aimed to identify and recognize best practices in K-12 arts education partnerships and foster their replication. A Steering Committee was formed,[5] and Jacqueline Guttman was appointed Project Director.

Then a third Board member, Robert Capanna, interceded with the Musical Fund Society in Philadelphia to enable us to get a grant of $5,000 for the upcoming Philadelphia conference. Bob was Executive Director of the Settlement Music School, which was the largest community music school in the country. He was one of the rising stars in the Guild. I developed great respect for his leadership abilities, his quick intelligence, and his willingness to lend a hand. I remember one year accosting him in the passage of a hotel a few hours before a conference session on fundraising and grant-writing. The presenter had not shown up and I asked him if he could help out. Without breaking a stride, he walked right into the meeting room ten minutes later, and gave an expert impromptu presentation. I could always count on his encouragement, support, and advice, which I valued highly. A brief quote from one of the many letters he wrote to me (see below) is symptomatic of the friendly, mutually constructive relationship we had before policy disagreements and other stresses in the late nineties created unfortunate tensions and eventually a rupture. The letter stands in stark contrast to the correspondence between us just five years later.

Bob Capanna to Lolita Mayadas 11/24/1993

You have my deepest admiration for your thoughtful professionalism and for your personal commitment and responsibility to the Guild. We all know a job is not just a job for a professional, but it is none the less gratifying, inspiring and reassuring to see and share the dedication that you and Azim so faithfully display with absolutely no fuss.

Rewinding to the eighties: our success in raising contributed revenues was becoming increasingly attributable to the efforts of Guild Trustees. Prior to 1983 three grants had been secured through the efforts of our Trustees. The first was from the Unger Foundation through Lester Glick, and others were from the North Carolina Council for the Arts and the Biddle Foundation through Henry Bridges. Both Lester and Henry had served as Presidents of the Board. But this latest effort by Board members at-large was something new. And several other Trustees, like Alvin (Skip) Reiss who wrote a monthly newsletter on the arts, were indispensable as resources, providing access to their connections and networks. This was exactly how the Board was supposed to function! In addition, the Board approved a motion requiring all Board members to make a minimum contribution of $75. [6]

The 1983 conference in Philadelphia was hosted by the Jenkintown Music School, which was headed by Monroe Levin. It was a joyous affair, further enlivened by Monroe's ebullient personality and quirky sense of humor. There was never an occasion that Monroe did not imbue the proceedings with a sort of comical insouciance. He had a lightness of touch, a keen sense of fun, and an ability not to take himself too seriously, which was very contagious and, curiously, very motivating.

It was at that conference that he introduced us to Jane Ballard, his Board President. She became a member of the Guild's Board the following year and later, President of the Board. A gracious and generous person, Jane was fully aware of her responsibilities as a Trustee and office bearer and set about making sure that all Board members, without exception, would make regular annual contributions to the Guild according to their means. To her goes the credit of formalizing the practice of mandatory board giving. She was ably joined in this effort by fellow Trustee Iona Benson. In spite of mixed results initially, this has become the *modus operandi* for Guild Board members albeit with different expectations for different categories.

The three-day conference was attended by some 150 people, which was a record for us. And we were honored that Frank Hodsoll, the Chairman of the National Endowment for the Arts, gave the keynote address. His presence provided a unique opportunity for Allen Sapp, Lester Glick, and Henry Bridges to have a luncheon meeting with him to discuss the Guild's future plans and NEA's possible support for a development campaign.

Monroe provided his own inimitable kickoff for the conference. Gathering everyone together at the base of the stairs at Jenkintown Music School, he mounted a few steps, baton in hand. He then passed out copies of this witty little libretto which he created for the occasion, and conducted us through a rousing rendition of the music for which it was set – the Hunters' Chorus from *Der Freischutz* by Carl Maria von Weber. It was the perfect rounding out of a successful year.

ALL OUR YESTERDAYS

Carl Maria von Weber: National Guild Song
(first sung at Jenkintown Music School's National Guild Evening, 11/14/83)

I.
In arts ed-u-cation
There's one organization
For all schools in the nation
And Canada, hooray,

That mails out its missiles
To poor school officials
Under these five initials:
"N G - C S A ".

Refrain
NG CSA CSA CSA CS
National Guild of
Community, -munity,
-munity, -munity,
National Guild of
Community Schools of the Arts.

II.
Now if you are in a fund drive
And you should need a
Couple Hundred thou,
Or if possibly you're seeking
A million bucks or two.

You just call Lolita
And tell her your problem
And if she can't help you
You know just where to sue.

III. (sung by the guests)
When last year we were in Charlotte
Tra-la, we danced all night
in stocking feet.
But this year we're at the mercy
Of all these opera nuts.

So here we are singing
Like fools in <u>Der Freischutz</u>
If - we were in costume
At least we'd have our rifle butts.

IV. (sung by the hosts)
Enough poetry and music,
For soon it will be breakfast capsule time
When all self-respecting Guild-ers
Are bright-eyed and alert.

So now that you've learned
To pronounce "Jenkintown" we will
Utter our fond farewells --
Next year we'll see you in Detrert.

Lolita Mayadas

Chapter Nine
Quo Vadis[1]

Let us hear your vision so we can more better do our job.

— George W. Bush[2]

The Guild had ended 1983 on a high note, rejoicing in the progress that had been made. All of us who attended the conference that year felt optimistic and exuberant by the time it ended – a mood reflected in a letter from the President Monroe Levin to all member schools:

> I want to thank those who took the trouble to send the many complimentary messages already received, which must have been written in a mood of great enthusiasm since they were mailed almost on arrival home. I'm glad to know that so many people had a good time in Philadelphia, and even happier to see how valuable the discussions and addresses proved to be.[3]

But later, when we came down to earth so to speak, it was obvious that none of our challenges had magically disappeared. We were still facing chronic issues of survival and sustainability, still trying to make both ends meet. Board members were still being urged to contribute their fair share, communication with the schools needed improvement, foundation grants were few and far between, governance structures needed to be strengthened, and shortfalls in revenues continued to occur. Reporting on the Guild's fiscal condition, Treasurer David Greer noted: "Though the financial situation has remained very stable since Lolita Mayadas joined the organization, a deficit …is anticipated for 1983/84." [4]

While contributed revenues continued to present an ongoing challenge, the good news was that proceeds from membership dues continued to increase as a result of rapid growth in the number of new members. The Board also opened the door to membership for schools operating as divisions of umbrella organizations. [5]

One question hovered over everything we did: where do we go from here? As Lewis Carroll said, "When you don't know where you are going, any road will take you there." [6] Without a road map, we were just putting one foot in front of the other – making up projects as we went along. Not surprisingly, some of those things led to dead ends.

But to our amazement, other program ideas clearly pointed the way forward for what was to come. Over the next ten years we were able to build upon those ideas, putting into place major national initiatives that were sustained through the support of private foundations and the NEA via their Challenge Grant Program. (These are referenced briefly below and described fully in ensuing chapters). Looking back, it could be argued that perhaps the Guild's greatest accomplishment over that decade was that it managed to earn the trust and cooperation of several key grant makers. But beyond that, those initiatives also led to a growing level of credibility for the field as a whole. At the time, such an outcome was not even imagined, let alone anticipated.

In the interim, we were having a ball, brainstorming about what we might do next. Listed below are just a few examples of the "sky's the limit" programs[7], some of which we shopped around to foundations in hopes of matching our goals with their interests. A sampling is given below:

- Regional Orchestra for visually and physically [disabled] students
- National Merit Award [for students at Guild schools]

- Research and Development of a pre-school comprehensive arts program

- Regional Master Classes by women artist/composers

- Publication of a national directory

- Film about Guild Schools and PSA's on video

- Leadership Seminars for School Board Members

- Teacher Training workshops

These program ideas were submitted in a statement to the Fundraising Committee. A note at the end of that statement declares cheerfully and with little heed for the demands of the job: detailed program descriptions and budgets are presently in preparation.

This was a classic case of programs chasing dollars. But miraculously, by October 1984, Board members had become excited enough that they opened the door to no less than twelve foundations resulting in at least three grants down the line. And by mid-February of the following year, the national office had submitted grant requests to eleven foundations as well as an Advancement Grant proposal to NEA. We expected, and received, a lot of turn-downs, but we learned eventually to use those as a way to build relationships.

It was clear that our primary tasks at this time were: 1) to secure the Guild financially and 2) to make it better known. How the latter goal was to be achieved remained an open question. In spite of its long history, few on the outside knew who we were and what we stood for. Conversely, insiders seemed to take pride in proclaiming loudly and often that the Guild was one of this country's best kept secrets. Many seemed to like it that way.

That perception of the Guild being some ʳ inevitably spilled over to member schools, wʰ claim they were unique, thinking to add vₐ appeals. But that approach only increased tʰ them from the unifying vision shared by ʳ indeed unique, but it was not alone.

For this and other reasons, the constituency of community schools remained a collection of single entities with no cohesive national voice, no national identity, no name recognition, no access to national resources, and nothing that visibly demonstrated what they stood for collectively. Their affiliation with the Guild was primarily of a social nature, and conferences were seen as an opportunity for catching up with old friends. In fact, in the early eighties the number of institutional members was still small enough to allow for bear hugs to be shared liberally amongst all present, thereby reinforcing the perception that the Guild was like a club. The idea that the Guild might somehow parlay its role as a service organization into one that provided leadership, visibility, and recognition for the field as a whole was neither understood nor envisioned.

Up to and including this point, the Guild had functioned primarily as an administrative partner to its members, serving as a clearinghouse for information. Like most other service organizations, we also offered internship programs, workshops, statistical surveys, newsletters, networking opportunities through local, regional, and national conferences, and advocacy for arts education through the Guild's participation in various national forums.

It must be said that advocacy received the least attention from the Guild at this point. The probable causes were lack of resources, skills and, I confess, some level of skepticism on my part. From that day to this I have never been able to figure out why the same advocacy strategies continue to be adopted year after year without ostensible result in the long run.

Unlike Marcy Horwitz and Ernie Dyson and later, Jonathan Herman, I was never comfortable with that part of my job which required me to take on the role of arts advocate. I did the best I could but my comfort level never improved. It seemed to me, then as now, that arts advocacy has turned into something of a Sisyphean dilemma where *cess is elusive and results uncertain. In spite of* *ed effort by all concerned, budget cuts to a greater* *degree seem to reappear with every new generation or change of administration. And the National Endowment for the Arts seems to be perpetually under siege. It is hard to know whether this situation will change, if ever, unless we take a radically new approach.*

There are so many leaders in business, the sciences, technology, and other non-arts professions for whom the arts have great intrinsic value and meaning. Here's a thought: could we not find a way to pull them all together into a national movement of sorts to speak on behalf of arts education for all? Their power would reside in their altruism and absence of self-interest. We made a miniscule start in this direction in 2000 when we organized a day-long symposium called "Arts Without Borders" in Los Angeles, my penultimate conference before I retired. Sadly, the idea did not survive.

One of the Guild's most important responsibilities was to strengthen the administrative capacity of its member institutions. With that in mind, we resurrected an earlier peer-to-peer informal service that paired directors of new and emerging schools with the leaders of older institutions. We depended entirely upon the time and expertise, which these established institutions so generously offered through their Trustees and staff. And even though participation on all sides was entirely voluntary, I do not know of a single instance where a request for advice was denied – no surprise since member schools had always been willing to share their expertise with each other.

The program turned out to be one of the most effective in the Guild's playbook because it tapped into the Guild's DNA, the sense that each school was invested in the wellbeing of the whole. It was later integrated into *GuildTech* and the New Arts Schools and Centers (NASCENT) programs through which established schools offered mentoring and technical assistance to new, emerging, and mid-sized institutions. Then, in the early nineties because of generous funding from the Lila Wallace-Reader's Digest Fund (now the Wallace Funds) and the NEA, the Guild was able to add some financial heft by providing grants to all participating schools.

Early in 1984, the Guild decided to revive its proposed Certificate Program after a hiatus of five years. The program had originally been proposed by Allen Sapp as a way of setting standards for graduating students at Guild schools and a means of preparing them for admission to college.

Now, a new Guild Certificate Committee, chaired by Helen Tuntland, was charged with formalizing this proposal. [8] A description and guidelines were sent out to all institutional members. Initially, several members expressed interest, especially in the New England region, but the response was generally desultory and the program was dropped by default.

Meanwhile, certification of member schools was moving forward as before. We had a long- established process whereby all applicants for institutional membership were evaluated against a specific set of criteria and, if approved, certified as members in one of three progressive categories: Provisional, Associate, and Full. The process entailed an initial application, site visit, recommendation by the Membership Committee, and a vote by the Board of Trustees. However, once certified, Full members were not required to go through a process of recertification.

The absence of a recertification process was viewed as problematic and led, a year later, to the formation of a Standards and Evaluation Committee with Robert Capanna (Chairman), Stephen Shapiro, Kalman Novak, and Allen Sapp. Their recommendations were a) that the initial evaluation should be a more thorough process, b) that all schools should be periodically re- evaluated, and c) that Full members should be re-evaluated five years after election. [9] The proposals remained "on the books" as it were but no further action was taken.

Several of our larger members were also accredited by the National Association of Schools of Music (NASM). It was a mutually beneficial arrangement, but it also led to some concern about competition in terms of membership recruitment. In fact, at one point several years later the Guild tried to put some teeth into its certification program by developing its own accreditation process. But it did not take us long to realize that this would have radically changed the

Guild's mission and its relationship with member schools and also that we lacked the resources and experience to carry it out.

A consensus emerged that the better course would be for NASM to press forward with a project already in the works: to develop a separate, though complementary, set of membership criteria specifically for community music schools. Such things tended to move slowly at NASM. In spite of diligent work by their non-degree granting commission (which included Guild representation), it took more than a decade before those criteria were finalized. In hindsight, it was just as well we pulled out of that arduous task.

In February 1984, Dr. Herbert Zipper announced to the Board that he wished to establish an annual composition prize for young composers with an endowment gift of $10,000. [10] The program was launched the following year with the title "Young Composers Awards." The first prize of $1,000 was named after Herbert Zipper. To support the second and third prizes, we approached the Lila Wallace-Reader's Digest Fund where we spoke for the first time with Jessica Chao, the Fund's Program Director. She wished us luck but turned us down since the program was outside the Foundation's interests. Herbert also approached Howard Klein, the Head of the Arts Department at Rockefeller Foundation, which he had led since 1973. Howard was an old friend of Herbert's and a long-time supporter of the National Guild, and he readily agreed to support three additional prizes with a grant of $2,750. [11]

Eight years later, Howard and Jessica would become key players in the development of the *GuildTech* program through the publication of their national study and two generous 3-year grants from the Lila Wallace-Reader's Digest Fund.

Soon after the February 4, 1984 Board meeting, Monroe Levin and I met NEA officials including Renee Levine, Director of the Inter-Arts Program, where renewal of the Guild's Development Grant was pending. [12] We were assured that our grant request of $15,000 would be favorably considered. We were also encouraged to apply for an Advancement Grant of $75,000. The standard dollar-to-dollar match would be required.

On the same day, we also met with Kamaki Kanahele at the Artists-in-Education program where we discussed the proposed New Jersey pilot project which we hoped would satisfy the Endowment's strong interest in partnership ideas. We received a cordial reception and, thankfully, the prospect of a $25,000 per year grant over a three-year period was viewed positively. Kamaki particularly liked the fact that we proposed to build on Herbert Zipper's original project in California, adding that "the idea of sending artists into the classroom to work with teachers on a long-term basis was something that had not been properly tried in the past."

The project we created in response to this meeting was the Arts Literacy Program in Newark Elementary Schools (ALPINES) in cooperation with Bill Reeder, Director of the Newark Community School of the Arts. We also received the support of the Victoria Foundation through successive grants for three years. ALPINES turned out to be a promising partnership model for other community schools to emulate. But in spite of Bill's extensive support on the ground, the Guild became too closely involved in day-to-day implementation. Also, the portion of the grant we retained for operating overhead nowhere near covered the actual cost.

It is said that experience is something you get just after you need it. We had learned never again to take on the job of project manager and fiscal agent for local programs. I vividly remember fighting traffic on the I-95 on my way down from Englewood to Newark several times a month, chafing at the tolls (no EZ Pass then), showing up at sundry meetings about logistics and minutiae that were outside my purview, and then heading back in time to hit the rush hour. Far better to have delegated those responsibilities.

On the other hand, by being present at meetings with artists and classroom teachers, we also learned about mutual expectations, concerns, and local needs – an invaluable lesson. It became obvious that the Guild would do better in future to act as catalyst and enabler – the germinator, as it were – for member schools to replicate partnerships on their own. We had made some mistakes, but our role in fostering partnerships had become clearer and the seeds for future dissemination of successful partnerships had been planted. And best of all, ALPINES ultimately evolved into the multi-year Partners in

Excellence Program launched in March 2000 with the generous support of the Josephine Bay Paul and C. Michael Paul Foundations (now the Bay and Paul Foundations).

We were making progress, but in terms of the visibility challenge, our programs and services to the field were not significant enough to serve as a basis for some great national attention-gathering enterprise. Sometimes it is necessary to break the mold. It seemed to me that what was needed was a major collaborative effort with our schools that would benefit the field as well as the Guild – something that could not fail to attract widespread attention and lead to significant exposure for the field. In brief, we needed to make a big and joyous splash…somehow.

But of course, it was not that simple. While there had been tangible improvement in the push to raise program grants and contributions, we were by no means out of the woods. In February 1984, [13] Monroe Levin thought it necessary to warn the Board about a projected shortfall of $7,000 in contributed income. Without additional funds the Guild would be unable to meet budgeted expenses by the end of the fiscal year in June 1984. Though several Trustees stepped up to the plate, the Guild still ended up with an operating deficit, leading to a reduced budget for the following year. The news was dispiriting even for the most optimistic among us. Mired as we were inside this chronic struggle to make ends meet, what possible chance could the "vision thing" have?

The answer would not be long in coming.

Lolita Mayadas

Chapter Ten
New Horizons

If all you ever do is all you've ever done then all you'll ever get is all you've ever got.

– Margaret Spellings[1]

By mid-1984 the location of the national office had turned into something of an embarrassment. While the Guild's move to our home in 1981 had taken place in response to a critical financial situation, we had managed to stabilize our operations to the point where we felt we could now afford independent offices. Besides, it was beyond time for this 47-year old organization to move out of the executive director's home. To have visitors (however rare) pick their way through our kitchen and descend the stairs between our refrigerator and the dishwasher down to the basement office hardly matched the image of the energetic and newly thriving organization we were trying to project. After a brief search for reasonably-priced premises, we moved out of one basement straight into another – this time to a lower-level two-room space in an office building at Cedar Lane, the main thoroughfare in Teaneck, New Jersey. Within two years, when the Guild was able to afford more appropriate premises, the office was moved to a spacious suite on the second floor of a building at 40 North Van Brunt Street, in Englewood, New Jersey, right next to the Performing Arts Center. And there we remained until the move to New York in 2002.

But now, for the first time in three years the Guild was obligated to pay rent, which inevitably created some strains on an already lean budget. There was general agreement that some cost- saving measures had to be implemented. The question was where and how. We were already operating very close to the bone, and there was virtually no fat we could cut out of the budget. At the same time, the Board was struggling to find the resources to hire an administrative assistant and to increase basic levels of compensation for staff. For my part, I was troubled when the Board authorized a salary raise for me personally without having a plan in place to acquire the dollars. However, one of the most encouraging developments in that fiscal year (1984-85) was that the Board set an aggregate goal of $4,000 in personal gifts – the largest amount to date.

At this point, Azim came up with the idea of changing his status from employee to consultant thereby saving the Guild the cost of his FICA contributions. [2] In addition, he offered to "assume the cost of one of the new office rooms…and [to use] it after hours for his own business. [3] This gesture halved the rental costs for the Guild and also lowered our line item expenses on benefits. The Board accepted these proposals and Azim was given the new title of Membership Consultant. His primary responsibility was to bring in 40 new institutional members during the current fiscal year (1984-85) – a goal he successfully achieved by increasing the number of institutional members from 120 in June 1984 to 160 in June 1985. His job also included "promoting and administering specific services to the field, development of chapters and organization and development of international membership and materials." For the first time in its long history, the Guild was looking to broaden its presence and outreach beyond these shores.

Meantime, the grants and contributions goal of $21,300 loomed large (approximately 23% of the budget). Without firm commitments from foundations in the prospect list or in the pipeline, that figure was entirely notional and represented nothing more than an attempt to balance the budget, which otherwise would have ended up firmly in the red. Eventually, the Board agreed to proceed "with all dispatch towards finding the ways and means to approve the budget in some form." At this point, in June 1984, their only option was to table approval of the budget to September 1984 with the understanding that salary increases would be retroactive to the start of the fiscal year in July 1984. [4]

A discussion also took place about increasing the number of board members to forty-five, and the Nominating Committee was asked to draft a rotation policy. Yet again, the pros and cons of having school directors on the Board came up, generating the usual lively and prolonged discussion. In the end, the desire to preserve diversity in terms of experience, skills, and resources (work, wisdom, and wealth in non-profit parlance) eventually prevailed, and the Board agreed to maintain the one-third/two-third representation of school professionals to lay members. We were greatly heartened that school directors seemed to be feeling more comfortable about nominating their own trustees to serve on the Guild's Board, thus reversing years of suspicion that this approach might lead to competition for personal contributions.

Towards the end of the meeting on June 2, 1984, someone reminded the Board that the Guild's 50th anniversary would occur in just three years. There was great excitement. What should be done to celebrate? Ideas abounded, but since there was little time to get into the details, Board President Monroe Levin offered to appoint a committee[5] to plan the 1987 event. Some, though not all of us, hoped it would be grand and splashy and attention-getting. Preliminary plans for the Celebration laid out some ambitious projects, including a History of the Guild, resuscitation of the Arts for All Fund (contingent upon the approval of NEA's Advancement Grant), a video documentary, a Gala Benefit Concert by Guild students and alumni at Carnegie Hall (presented as a joint fundraiser), a joint schools marathon concert (including dance), a luncheon honoring past presidents, a dinner inviting prominent philanthropic leaders, and an exhibition of art work by Guild school students. Later, we added the publication of a full-page ad in *The New York Times*, promoting community schools. We hoped that all member schools would contribute to this effort. By June 1986, a detailed budget had been developed with revenues projected at $60,000 and estimated expenses of $35,000. I recall that the Carnegie Hall rental at that time plus labor costs totaled $15,000, a steal in terms of today's dollars, but it represented a huge commitment on the part of the Guild at that time.

On June 14, 1984, Monroe sent an invitation to Board members to attend a special get-together with Herbert Zipper on June 27th. "I hope this event will find more than a few Board Trustees available and that Dr. Zipper's long and vital association with the Guild will prove especially helpful at this time of sudden expansion and increasing national importance." Seven Guild Trustees attended and had a chance to brainstorm with Herbert about the Guild's goals and purposes in hopes of drawing up a new case statement that summer.

A timely reminder about the 50th anniversary occurred at the November 11, 1984, Board meeting when Trustee Robert Egan announced his plans to write the history of the National Guild to be published in time for the anniversary. He would begin his research, he said, by sending out a questionnaire to all member schools. The book was eventually published by the Scarecrow Press in 1989 with the name: *Music and the Arts in the Community: The Community Music School in America*. As the name suggests, it was more a history of the movement rather than the Guild.

Meantime, our efforts to connect with other international associations and individuals in the field of music education were beginning to bear fruit. In May 1984, Azim attended the International Society of Music Education (ISME) conference at Eugene, Oregon, where he was introduced to Dr. Diethard Wücher, President of the *Verband deutscher Musikschulen* (VdM), the professional association for some 900 music schools in Germany.[6] Dr. Wücher was intrigued and excited by the Guild, and not long thereafter he invited us to send ensembles from up to 10 member schools to the Fourth European Youth Festival to celebrate the International Year of Youth, so named by the United Nations. The Festival also marked the tercentenaries of Bach, Handel, and Scarlatti.

All expenses and accommodation within Germany were to be provided by the hosts. Needless to say, we accepted his invitation with alacrity. And we reciprocated by inviting Dr. Wücher to attend the upcoming Board meeting.

Asked to say a few words at the meeting on November 11, 1984, in Detroit, Dr. Wücher presented three proposals to the Board for Guild affiliation with an international guild he wished to establish. The proposals were referred by the Board to an ad hoc committee for further study. The meeting was also attended by the Israeli musician Ophra Broshi.

Both Diethard and Ophra attended the national conference in Detroit that year as well as the Annual Meeting on November 12, 1984. A third guest was Stefán Edelstein, Director of the association of Icelandic Community Music Schools. All three spoke briefly about their own institutions. But needless to say, we were all captivated by Dr. Wücher's enthusiasm about the upcoming events in Germany including the concurrent conference of the European Union of Music Schools (EMU), which I was invited to attend.

We followed through without delay and sent out a note to our member schools to find out if they would be interested in attending the Youth Festival. Ten schools responded positively, but eventually 8 ensembles[7] with some 225 students confirmed their participation. They were the only groups from the US to be invited.

By early 1985, as a result of intense effort, fundraising had picked up significantly. By January 1985 a total of $67,750 from eleven public and private grant-makers had been received to support the Guild's programs including the NEA's Artists-in-Education Program, the Exxon Corporation, Helena Rubinstein Foundation, and others. We were especially pleased to receive renewals of grants, albeit in diminishing amounts, from the NEA's Inter-Arts Division, the Charles Ulrick and Josephine Bay Foundation, and the Rockefeller Foundation.[8] At least six additional foundations and/or corporations had agreed to consider proposals from the Guild, and six others were placed in the promising prospects list. A major Advancement grant proposal was also in the pipeline. Donations from individual members had improved, and gifts and pledges from the Board had increased to $5,000. Best of all, Board members were putting themselves out for this effort, visiting potential grant makers either on their own or together with the Executive Director.

Not to be outdone, earned revenue as a result of membership recruitment was more than keeping pace. A new category called Seasonal Arts Schools for 6-week summer schools was introduced. Further, in an attempt to "stand behind" current claims of quality and accessibility, a new proposal was floated to re-evaluate current member schools. [9] Although that idea was eventually turned down, it cleared the path for the Guild to work in cooperation with the National Association of Schools of Music to accredit non-degree-granting member schools through a joint program. A new and expanded chapter structure was also in place.

Administratively, the Guild seemed to have attained a more formal and predictable structure. There were regular reports from the Executive Director at each Board meeting and, more notably, reports from each committee. Goals, strategies, targets, and results were spelled out for review by the Board. All this looked very good on paper. But in most cases, sheer logistics prevented regular committee meetings, and it fell to staff to fill in the holes and prepare reports. In spite of best intentions, the problem was not much different from that which triggered Marcy Horwitz's lament five years earlier when she expressed "increasing anxiety about operational procedures, namely, that some committees were not pulling their weight." [10] We were making progress but clearly, we still had a long way to go in this area.

In real terms, it seemed that the Guild might have found an acceptable balance between income from membership dues, program grants, and contributed revenues. Unrestricted grants for operating support were minimal. However, each program grant yielded 15-20% for operating overhead which was helpful to the bottom line. All this was cause for celebration. But it was too soon to break out the champagne. In spite of these successes, the sustainability issue still loomed over all our deliberations. It remained the ever-present elephant in the room for a decade or more.

But we didn't have time to think about that. We were just too preoccupied with arrangements for the trip to the European Youth Festival to worry about phantom elephants or survival issues. The excitement was palpable, and we were all eagerly looking forward to the first-ever international trip by member school students under the aegis of the Guild.

So, one beautiful spring morning in May 1985, I, in my capacity as Executive Director of the Guild, set off for Germany, sharing a plane with a young ensemble from Chicago's Merit Music School, Bernice Ransley, its Program Director, and sundry chaperones. Each of the eight participating ensembles had been assigned to a German partner music school. The mood was as joyous as any field trip and the kids never seemed to run out of steam.

The opening concerts took place in Munich on May 24 and included the Levine School of Music, Washington, DC, and their partner school, the Peter Cornelius Conservatory in Mainz, conducted by Michael Morgan. The evening closed with a concert at Olympia Halle followed by a huge "Europarty" for 9,000 youngsters from 23 countries. There was a moment of panic when the buses picked up the students at the end, and we discovered that one student from the Merit Music Program had gone missing. Fortunately, the boy was found by a police officer and promptly returned to base.

On the following day, in perfect weather, each joint ensemble had the opportunity of performing in the open air at 40 locations in Munich, including the Marienplatz, the English Gardens, the St. Johannes Kirsche, the Victualmarkt, and so on. It was fun to watch so many young people playing in concerts together, hanging out together, and trying to talk to each other in some combination of language and gesture. Everyone seemed to be thoroughly enjoying the experience even though the kids had to spend the night in sleeping bags on the floor of Germany's many "gymnasiums." All the rest of us were assigned to hotels. But Kal Novak, who was the Director of Music Center of the North Shore, and the conductor of their orchestra, firmly refused hotel accommodations and insisted on sleeping on the floor with his kids.

The closing concert at the Olympic Stadium lasted more than three hours and included one ensemble from each country with the US being represented by the Joyeux Wind Ensemble from The Colburn School in Los Angeles, conducted by Yehuda Gilad. It was attended by Germany's President, Richard von Weiszäcker, who said in his closing address (simultaneously translated into several languages): "Music not only surmounts linguistic barriers. Can there be anything more gratifying for those singing and playing, listening and applauding here than the fact that people from 23 countries give each other pleasure? Your performance shows that pleasure does not come about through inaction…but through the readiness to attune oneself to others and work together with them." At the end of the program, some 15,000 members of the audience joined hands and sang "Auld Lang Syne" followed by a rousing performance of Beethoven's "Ode to Joy" from his Ninth Symphony by the international orchestra and joint chorus assembled from all the schools. The occasion was a fitting end to a memorable festival. At a private reception before this event, I was presented to the German President and his wife, and I also had the chance to meet the Chinese Minister of Culture, who asked me to pass on his warmest regards to Herbert Zipper.

The conference of the European Union of Music Schools (EMU) was also being held concurrently with the Festival. We were housed at what looked like a former monastery in Marktoberdorf set in the beautiful countryside of the Black Forest near Munich. I remember being woken in the morning by the bells of cows grazing outside in the verdant fields! I was happy that Gary Zeller, Director of the MacPhail Center for the Arts and International Committee Member, was also there. There was unanimous agreement that EMU and the Guild attempt to cooperate for the purpose of promoting music, the performing arts, and education in Europe and America wherever financially possible. A joint declaration to this effect was duly issued to the press at the conclusion.

It almost goes without saying that the Festival and conference brought the Guild to the attention of many European educators who had never heard of community schools in the United States; the hope was that this initiative would be the beginning of further dialogue and exchanges between the Guild and European schools. This was advocacy on a scale we could not have anticipated or even imagined, and it allowed the Guild to think outside the box. It also gave us the confidence to pursue other large initiatives, some of which turned out to be more controversial than others.

Chapter Eleven
Nothing Ventured, Nothing Gained

If at first the idea is not absurd then there is no hope for it.

– Albert Einstein

"You're going to sink the Guild," said David Greer severely, turning to me. The remark was greeted with general pandemonium and repeated calls for order. The occasion was a Board meeting where the central agenda item was the National Festival of the Arts to celebrate the Guild's 50th anniversary in 1987. David's ominous warning specifically referred to the projected Gala concert at Carnegie Hall featuring an orchestra composed entirely of gifted students from Guild member schools and the participation of distinguished artists. The concert was to be the signature event in a three-part celebration in New York, which was intended to showcase what community schools do in a tangible way. The idea for that concert was actually suggested by Mitch Miller during the course of expanding the Guild's National Advisory Council. The other two events planned were a six-hour Wall to Wall concert featuring a series of music and dance performances at Symphony Space by students representing the great majority of students attending community schools, and an Art Exhibit at the Penta Hotel (the site of the conference).

David's opinion was shared by Hadassah Markson for the same reasons. Their primary concern was the challenge of filling the 3,000-seat auditorium at Carnegie Hall. They felt this would be an impossible task, even though it was to be presented as a joint fundraiser, i.e. member schools would be encouraged to buy tickets in bulk at a generous discount but would be permitted to sell them at face value, keeping the difference. We hoped this approach would reduce the risk for all concerned. In fact, this plan to share proceeds was considered to be an "important catalyst" for the schools. [1] But neither David nor Hadassah believed that the pride felt by schools whose students were chosen to participate in this prestigious event would be a sufficient motivator nationwide.

David Greer was the founder-director of the Bloomingdale House of Music in New York, and a long-time member of the Guild's Board. He also served as Treasurer for many years. A slight, slim man, he had the sweetest of natures and the most infectious little giggle I have ever encountered. To say he was lovable would be an understatement. But he was also very cautious by nature and would fret over a discrepancy of even a couple of cents in any budgetary report. So for him, the festival was a financial challenge of massive proportions and a risky and irresponsible proposal on my part. He probably lost a lot of sleep over it.

Hadassah Markson too had been a long-time member of the Guild's Board and served as Secretary and Vice-President. She was the Director of the 92nd Street Y School of Music, which had been founded by her father in 1919, on New York's Upper East Side. She took over his Director position after he died. I recall that before joining the Guild, I had been looking around for a part-time position in New York, but I didn't have a network or any connections, having lived in other states and cities for more than six years after my family and I emigrated from India.

I was, however, referred to Stowe Phelps who was, at that time, Head of the Board at Third Street Settlement Music School. He was very helpful and suggested I call Hadassah. "She knows everybody!" he said. So, of course I reached out to her, and that was the start of a long and wonderful friendship between us. In fact, I learned I could count on her loyal support and advice at all times, good or bad. I believe the Carnegie Hall Concert was the first and last time we disagreed so vehemently.

As for the Board meeting which created such a furor, fortunately there were many other leading members of the Board (including Monroe Levin, the President), who thought that the Festival could, and should, take place for many reasons, including increased name recognition and publicity for what had long been considered a "best kept secret." Fortunately, they were vocal in their support, and Betty Allen was appointed Co-Chair of the Carnegie Hall Committee. She was joined by Ajit Hutheesing, Chairman of the Board of the Sherwood Capital Corporation, who also agreed to serve as Co-Chair of the Gala Celebration. Ajit was a member of a prominent family in India and an old friend of Lolita's. He was well connected and we hoped he would open some doors for us. That hope was not unfounded. He introduced us to Maestro Zubin Mehta, who accepted the position of Honorary Chair of the Gala Celebration and recorded a special video, and also to James Wolfensohn, Chairman of the Board of Trustees at Carnegie Hall, and later, President of the World Bank. James subsequently became Chairman of the Board of the John F. Kennedy Center for the Performing Arts. In that capacity, he allowed the Guild the use of their auditorium on a pro bono basis for the next National Festival in November 1997, an act of extraordinary generosity. It should be said that James was a gifted cellist who studied for a time with Jacqueline Du Pre. [2] For him, music was a great and abiding passion.

In the midst of all this excitement, a report dated May 21, 1987, from Bob Capanna, Chair of the Accreditation Committee, noted: "In the brief life of this committee, it has become clear that there is little support for the idea of the Guild granting accreditation." He added, "There are several arguments against accreditation: that it is an inappropriate function for the Guild, and would be a usurpation of another organization's domain; that it is philosophically inappropriate to implement uniform quality standards across a diverse community-based constituency."

Meantime, we had some exciting news about the participation of well-known artists in the Carnegie Hall event: Wynton Marsalis agreed to perform with the Harlem Boys Choir and Maestro Joseph Silverstein consented to conduct the specially formed National Guild Youth Symphony consisting of over 100 students chosen by blind audition from thirty-nine community schools from all over the country. By early October, $20 tickets had been sold out and there was limited availability of $15 tickets. We had also taken out a full-page ad in *The New York Times* supported by contributions from member schools. The title was: "A celebration of 50 years of arts in the community." A listing of all member schools followed, together with messages and photos of participating V.I.P's in the world of music and the arts including Zubin Mehta, Wynton Marsalis, Kitty Carlisle Hart, Joseph Silverstein, and Leonard Pennario. The ad was reproduced as a large poster and placed under the marquee at Carnegie Hall. It now hangs on the wall at the entrance to the Guild's New York office. A copy will be found at the end of this chapter.

By the time of the concert at Carnegie Hall on November 8, 1987, we were all in a state of nervous anticipation, not being quite certain how it would all turn out. But arriving at the hall that morning for the first rehearsal, I found Hadassah and David, who was grinning from ear to ear. He had tears of joy in his eyes at the incredible prospect of a student from his school performing on the stage of Carnegie Hall. I was touched by their enthusiasm and tacit acknowledgement that their initial skepticism was perhaps unjustified. It was truly inspiring for all of us to see so many young players from all over the country tuning up and chatting happily with each other.

Many years later, the cellist Wendy Warner (representing the Music Center of the North Shore, Winnetka, Illinois) told us that the event was one of the highlights of her life. No doubt that reaction was shared by many others whose participation added some glitter to burgeoning resumes. That day, we watched in awe as chartered buses arrived from points near and far, all of them filled with school trustees and performers plus sundry relatives including parents, grandparents, aunts, and uncles. All were only too happy to cheer on their talented children. Much to our delight the hall was about three-quarters full by the time the program began, with barely an empty seat in the orchestra section. For the sake of prudence, we had closed off the balcony. The largest contingent from a single school came from Philadelphia's Settlement Music School (Executive Director, Robert Capanna) with just under 100 people.

For all the success of the Carnegie Hall concert there were, however, some sour notes about the other events. For instance, there was criticism about the Wall to Wall Concert (or Performathon) amid the perception that it had been relegated to secondary status. Also, the Art Exhibit was said to be insufficiently publicized. Regardless, the Festival was considered to be a remarkable success overall both artistically and financially. It netted $40,000 for the National Guild.[3]

There are no statistics to prove this, but the publicity generated by the entire Celebration probably helped bring Guild schools to the attention of a greater public as well as important grant-makers.

Chapter Twelve
Process and Product

Chance favors the prepared mind.

– Louis Pasteur

It was not long before the exuberance of that grand celebration morphed into cold reality and a more introspective mode. As a result, after years of creating programs on a somewhat ad hoc basis, the Board now decided that it was past time for the Guild to develop a more organized approach to its programs and services to the field. As a result, the Guild's first Board Retreat took place March 4-6, 1988, with Halsey and Alice North as facilitators, prior to the development of a Strategic Plan. The Retreat was supported by the Mary Flagler Cary Charitable Trust through the kind intercession of their Program Director Gayle Morgan, who later joined the Guild's Board. The stated purpose of the Retreat was to enable the Board to determine the goals and strategies for the National Guild over the next five years.

To begin with, the Board reviewed the Guild's mission, the role of board and committees, and an overview of the Guild's constituency, membership, programs, and services. Several small committees were formed to work on different aspects of the agenda and were charged with making their recommendations to the entire Board at the end of the day.

By the close of the Retreat, a number of goals had been identified and ways to achieve those goals spelled out. As Jane Ballard, Board President, wrote in her note to absent members, the Retreat was "exciting and exhilarating and a great success. Under

Halsey and Alice North's guiding hands we explored every aspect of the Guild and emerged with a real sense of what we are about and where and how we, as a Board, feel we should go." She added, "The most dramatic and exciting event was [Trustee] Bill Dahling's unexpected $12,000 challenge." The money was to be used to pay for extra office help and travel by the Executive Director for visits to Guild schools while the match would be applied to operating expenses. Miraculously, by Sunday noon the Board had pledged $9,250 toward the challenge.

A new mission statement was also approved as follows:

The purpose of the National Guild of Community Schools of the Arts is to foster, nurture and encourage high quality arts education designed to meet community needs and to provide services and programs for the benefit of its members.

Just a year later, in February 1989, the Guild started to consider yet another possible name change. Suggestions put forward were:

- Community Arts America, the National Guild of Community Schools of the Arts

- Community Arts Schools of America

- National Association of Community Arts Schools (or National Association of Community Schools of the Arts)

However, no consensus could be reached immediately about an appropriate choice of name, and the Board decided to table further consideration of this issue.

A month later, at an Orientation Meeting for new Board members on March 3, 1989, Lolita Mayadas presented an outline of the state of the Guild, including a description of current programs and services, as follows:

- Annual Conference

- Regional meetings of member schools organized by local chapters once each year

- Arts Management in Community Institutions (AMICI), a two-week hands-on seminar and training program started in 1985 for schools less than 5 years old, led by Andrea Olin Gomes Kaiser.

- Publication of a range of resource materials, including the annual Membership Directory, the monthly *Guildnotes* newsletter, and how-to manuals

- *GuildTech* – an informal institutional mentoring program whereby emerging schools were paired with established institutions for the purpose of soliciting advice and counseling

- Implementation of the New Arts Schools and Centers Program (NASCENT) whose purpose was to support the start-up of new community schools of the arts in communities where they do not exist.

- International Student Exchange Program begun in 1985 in conjunction with the European Youth Festival that year

- Young Composers Awards Competition

- Resale of *Kindermusik* materials for profit under the name of *Tonekinder*. (This program was short-lived primarily because of objections from member schools which felt that the Guild should not be in the business of promoting or endorsing educational materials).

A Benefit Raffle had also been introduced to support the costs of hiring a new staff person, but that, too, was cancelled after one year.

At this point, the Guild had 176 member schools and a budget of just under $200,000. Earned Revenues from Membership Dues represented about 25% of the $195,000 budget for fiscal year 1989/90. But to achieve annual goals for grants and contributions was a constant struggle.

Lolita Mayadas

While the Board Retreat had focused on Programs and Services and on the role of the Board, by and large the Guild was still chugging along at a frustratingly slow pace and living more on hope than reality. But things were about to change dramatically in a way no one could possibly have anticipated.

Chapter Thirteen
Field of Dreams[1]

Well, the Fund is impressed.

– Jessica Chao[2]

In April 1990, Gayle Morgan, Program Director, Mary Flagler Cary Charitable Trust and Rachel Bellow, Program Director, Andrew W. Mellon Foundation offered to arrange an informational meeting in New York to introduce the Guild to other funders.[3] The purpose of the presentation was to "talk about collaborative arts education programs that are currently in place in the public schools, utilizing the resources of community arts schools." It was attended by eleven major national foundation officers and a group of Guild school directors. Little did either Gayle or Rachel realize what they had set in motion because this was the first time that Jessica Chao, Program Director of the Lila Wallace-Reader's Digest Fund, was formally introduced to the National Guild. Two years earlier, John Zinsser, a friend of Guild President Jane Ballard, had sent out feelers to some of his personal contacts at the Fund to seek their support for the Guild and two modest proposals were submitted.[4] But neither one was funded.

Years later, Jessica wrote me a letter:

"I remember thinking how wonderful that there's a national organization trying to herd these very important, very independent community organizations — important for communities, important for young people, for education, and for arts education. I was also impressed with you and what you were trying to accomplish. I remember thinking that your organization and your members needed support for infrastructure. [And] I did enjoy working with you and your husband…so, so many years ago."[5]

And then, one stunning summer morning in 1990, I got a call out of the blue from our old friend Howard Klein. "Lolita," he said, "I am in Jessica Chao's office and they want to know if you would be interested in having them carry out a national study of the field." I almost fell out of my chair. I had been trying to get their interest in supporting our Young Composers Awards Program but without success. But this was something else entirely. "Are you kidding, Howard?" I said. "Of course we would be interested!"

By the fall of 1990, the Fund's initial inquiry had firmed up to the point that Jessica suggested a presentation at the Annual Meeting of the National Guild in Boston that November. There she announced the appointment of a Study Team consisting of Howard Klein, Richard Evans, and Jane Delgado. To begin with, Dr. Herbert Zipper explained that an entirely new project was about to be launched that would be of the utmost significance to the Guild and to the cultural needs of this country. He concluded by introducing Howard Klein.

Howard Klein, who had overseen the arts programs at the Rockefeller Foundation for nineteen years, had decided to take early retirement and left the organization in 1992. I had first met him face to face about five years earlier. His appearance reminded me of one of those noblemen in a Dutch painting. Sporting a small goatee beard, he was a genial man with a ready smile and an amicable temperament. There was not a trace of arrogance in him, in spite of his stellar reputation and awesome intellectual capabilities. He was a polymath, able to converse with knowledge and depth about everything from Zen Buddhism to philosophy to Indian ragas– a truly Renaissance man and a joyous one at that. Every conversation I had with him enriched and expanded my understanding of the world we live in. And I must confess that I miss them. Besides, he had been a consistent and articulate supporter of the

Guild's work for decades and for that we offer him our profound thanks.

At the outset of his remarks, Howard recognized Jessica Chao, whose support had enabled the process to begin. He hoped, he said, that it would attract the attention of other funders. Richard and Jane then outlined the shape of the research, the basis of the survey, and the method to be followed. They urged that all Guild members make a point of returning their surveys and asked the schools to identify school trustees and other community leaders who would be able to meet with the Study Team. Jane particularly asked for input into what their vision for the future might be.

And then it was Jessica's turn at the lectern.

After an introduction by Jane Ballard, President of the National Guild's Board, Jessica eloquently explained the rationale behind the Fund's decision to study the field and said that the mission of the Fund was to "promote the growth and appreciation of the arts in America through projects of national impact in the performing, literary, and visual arts." With an annual budget of approximately $20 million, she added, "the Fund is particularly interested in the relationship between the arts and the community, the building of bridges between these entities, and the restoration of "community." In closing, she emphasized that the Fund wanted to learn what it could do to help Guild schools become more effective as community cultural centers.

By the time of the Board meeting on June 22, 1991, the outlook for a positive outcome had improved significantly. Feedback from the Study Team showed that they had been very favorably impressed with what they had seen during their visits to 30 schools. And I pointed out to the Board [6] that Jessica was most encouraging about supporting the Guild itself as well as the field of community arts schools as a whole. In fact, soon afterward the Fund invited the Guild to submit a proposal. Being an optimist, I was hopeful they would support us in a substantial way. But my fingers remained firmly crossed! I need not have worried. The ball had started to roll in earnest.

After many meetings and several drafts, the Guild submitted an application for a three-year, $623,000 grant to enhance and expand the *GuildTech* Program of technical assistance and managerial consulting.[7] The proposal was approved and funded in full on September 26, 1991, by the Board of the Lila Wallace-Reader's Digest Fund, and announced in November 1991 at the Guild's national conference at St. Louis, MO.

In addition to *GuildTech,* the Fund also announced a program of direct support (estimated to be in the range of $4,000,000) to community schools of the arts. Some 20 schools would be invited to submit proposals for grants ranging from $150,000 to $750,000 to support scholarships and/or faculty development. All grants would require a 1:1 match.

This announcement was greeted with spontaneous applause and great excitement. And sure enough, the next day, on November 16, 1991, after initial introductions, Howard Klein went into considerable detail as to the reason for the Fund's interest in community schools of the arts. He began by citing the key factors in selecting these schools: they provide open access, they encompass all ages, and they place high value on motivation and less on talent. He added that the context of the Study was the background of the worsening position of arts education in the public sector. Using slides to illustrate his text, he provided a thorough and comprehensive analysis of the climate in which community schools of the arts were functioning.

Jane Delgado then addressed the problems of administration in Guild schools, the level of staffing, and issues confronting faculty. Also using slides, she provided an analysis of the various stages from conception to realization in the development of individual schools.

Richard Evans, who led the project as a whole and authored the Study, then spoke about the finances of Guild schools — where the financing comes from and how the money was being spent.[8] Richard knew the subject intimately, for it was he who devised the survey of Guild members, analyzed the survey results (narrative and quantitative), and led the site visits (some in combination with Howard and Jane). Through charts, he outlined the financial profile of community schools of the arts. He also presented an analysis of their aggregate figures in comparison with other arts organizations and emphasized that much work needed to be done to increase private sector support for the field.

Wrapping up on behalf of the Study team, Howard Klein expressed his gratitude to Jane Delgado for introducing the human element to otherwise dry material. He pointed out that all three members of the team had been deeply moved and inspired by their visits to the schools. And he drew particular attention to the imagination of faculty and staff, all of whom seemed to be totally undeterred by actual resources at hand, or lack thereof. He explained that motivation seemed to be the driving force behind their commitment to the school's mission. Likewise, the students' desire to learn convincingly demonstrated the primacy of motivation over what is generally regarded as "the talented." Howard also recognized that Guild schools were deeply imbedded in their communities and announced that the Study attempted to acknowledge that fact with its title, which was taken from an Emily Dickinson poem: "Lay the laurel wreath on one too intrinsic for renown." [9] He closed by saying that the schools were intrinsic, but must work for renown. At the same time, he also pointed out the enormous challenge faced by the Guild in terms of reaching into large, underserved areas of the country.

Concluding the session, Jessica Chao then thanked Howard Klein and also Lolita Mayadas for her invitation. Jessica's remarks are inserted below, verbatim:

> Just about this time last year, we announced that the Lila Wallace-Reader's Digest Fund was commissioning a survey on you and your colleagues. I'm pleased that we were able to share with you some of the results of that research today. Howard, Richard and Jane have been poring over every minute detail of what makes a community school of the arts work, and what makes it unique. And they've been feeding this information to us at the Fund. Well, the Fund is impressed. There has been a noisy and troublesome debate which has been rippling through the arts community in recent years. It's been a fabricated battle between quality and access. And there's

you, striving for nothing less than both quality and access, very quietly…

Today, on behalf of the Staff and the Board of the Lila Wallace-Reader's Digest Fund, I would like to announce our first step in supporting your field. The Fund has awarded the National Guild of Community Schools of the Arts a grant of $623,000 over three years to sponsor *GuildTech,* a consolidation, upgrading, and expansion of technical assistance services, designed to help you do what you do best.

In the coming months, Lolita and her staff will keep you updated on the services. There's some material on *GuildTech* on the table. I hope you'll participate. The Fund also plans to expand its support of this field, and expects to announce a pilot program of direct support [to] schools in the spring. For the pilot phase, a limited number of the most established and largest schools have been invited to submit proposals. Based on the success of these schools, and this pilot phase, the Fund will then design its future relationship in this field. So, do wish your colleagues great success in the next few months.

The work of the community schools of the arts [over] the past decade has been extraordinary, demonstrating the magnitude of grass roots participation in the arts. The Fund hopes that by strengthening this field, we'll be increasing community access to the worlds of music, dance, theatre, and the visual arts. I congratulate Lolita, her staff and the Board of the Guild. Thank you.

I would be remiss if I did not say a personal word of commendation here about Jessica Chao. I consider myself lucky to have worked with her for many, many reasons. As we tackled multiple drafts of the proposal together, she was always ready with helpful suggestions and guidance. But anything woolly or inexact didn't have a chance of getting by her virtual blue pencil. She was a mentor, a constructive critic, and a wonderful friend. Her voice was invaluable in shaping the GuildTech grant. And if it is true that, in time, I became a reasonably effective grant writer, I owe that skill entirely to Jessica's input and advice. I learned more from her than perhaps she herself realized. And I have thought many times since then that this was the paradigm for what a partnership with a supportive funder should look like.

The Study team also announced at the Board meeting on November 17, 1991, that the Fund was interested in ensuring the long-term stability and growth of the Guild. With that goal in mind, they made available the services of Richard Evans and Jane Delgado for a period of six months to assist the Guild in the process of institutional development.

On behalf of everyone, Jane Ballard thanked Jessica, Howard, Richard, and Jane for the recognition that they were giving to this field, for putting the Guild in the spotlight, and for helping the Guild "in the most practical way we could ever imagine!"

Carl Atkins, the new Board President, then added his thanks to the Study Team and the Fund. But before adjourning, he invited everyone to join in a surprise celebration and tribute to Lolita Mayadas for "ten years of wonderful service and leadership and for bringing to fruition this particular project." [10] At this point, a cake was produced with 10 candles which were lit by Jessica, who entered enthusiastically into the spirit of the occasion.

And just after blowing out the candles I thanked everyone very much for this wonderful surprise, and then made a wish that the next decade would enable the Guild to "have our cake and eat it too!"

Earlier that year an article in *The New York Times* [11] headed "Wallace Fund Quietly Grows Into Nation's Top Arts Donor" by William Grimes offered some quotes and comments: " 'The Lila Wallace-Reader's Fund is about 8 on a scale of 10 as far as difficulty in getting a grant,' said Anthony C. Tapia, program director of the Association of Performing Arts Presenters in Washington. 'The idea of partnership is essential,' he continued, 'and applicants really need to demonstrate that. They have to show they are creating links in the community on a long-term basis.'[12]

"After signing the checks, however, the Fund steps out of the way. 'Once they have the grant,' said Jessica Chao, '[the grantees] make the decisions, because they're better at it than we are. The artist throws it out there, and the community responds. Sometimes it works, sometimes it doesn't. Ultimately, what the money cannot do is much greater than what it can do,' she continued. 'But it can give that little incentive that then allows all those creative people in the field to fill in everything that money cannot do.'" [13]

The following excerpts from the published Introduction to the Study spell out the history and background of privately funded arts education and the rationale for selecting Guild members for eventual support.

> With the public school system unable to act as the stable center for basic arts instruction, strength of demand for arts education has helped to fuel the creation of other, complementary educational venues. Major cities, facing declining revenues and increasing need, have cut programs in the arts....As this has been happening, a growing number of communities have seen the development, within and outside the public schools, of new institutions dedicated specifically to providing professional arts instruction to school-age children, as well as to students of pre- or post-school age. These institutions have come into being at an increasing rate over the last 30 years.

> The diversity of institutions and educational philosophies that has arisen may be illustrated by considering a specific grouping that emerged in the 1980s [which led to the] establishment in 1983 of the Network of Performing and Visual Arts Schools....While the Network "strives to inspire and maintain excellence in arts education" (in the words of its mission statement) it does not see its role as

screening or evaluating its membership. It is therefore principally an advocacy and communications network, offering opportunities for discussion and information exchange between widely disparate organizations....But [that characteristic] and the underlying emphasis on selecting the gifted and talented, meant that its membership was of no particular assistance to the Study Team in pursuing the goals of the Lila Wallace-Reader's Digest Fund – to identify a coherent universe of schools offering exemplary open access.

Seeking further information on arts schools that offer community access to quality arts instruction outside the public education system, the Study Team surveyed a total of 333 institutions from November 1990 to March 1991. The survey included a detailed questionnaire sent to the 183 United States schools (independent and divisional) that were at that time in membership of the National Guild of Community Schools of the Arts....The 93 members that responded ...declared a policy of open access to a community of all ages, and at all stages of artistic development. From their response we found these institutions to have fundamental and important characteristics in common, through which they are genuinely linked as a national movement. We learned that it was therefore appropriate to separate them from most of the other arts schools we surveyed and to consider them for further study as a group apart.

The Guild schools share many other common features, as we shall see...what sets the community schools apart from most of the others we surveyed is, first of all, their primary commitment to providing high quality sequential learning programs in the arts, through concentrating on individual practical instruction; more specifically, these schools recognize that, in the development of individual ability in the arts, motivation and commitment on their own can stimulate the emergence of latent talent. As the cornerstone of successful teaching, this concept has led them to adopt a uniform admissions policy.

Among all the private nonprofit providers of practical and historical arts education that we reviewed, we found that the community schools offer to their communities a panoply of services unmatched by others....Articulating a long tradition, community schools remain at the grass roots. They have not as a group been heralded for their contribution, but have blended quietly into their communities, attracting little support or acknowledgement outside their immediate environment. Our intention in this report is to help make a good community school recognizable, by highlighting the features that are to be found, the achievements that might be expected, and the hazards to be faced.

Capping it off in the Executive Summary, Christine De Vita, President of the Lila Wallace- Reader's Digest Fund, noted: "It is our hope that this report stimulates interest in the community arts education movement and that both the public and private sectors of our country will recognize and support the tremendous contributions these schools are making to the communities across America."

And sure enough, in June 1992 the Lila Wallace-Reader's Digest Fund announced the names of the first nine schools to receive a total of $3.17 million over three years in direct support.[14]

Interestingly, all nine schools were members of the National Guild and would use a portion of their grants to broaden access to arts instruction and to maintain and increase the quality of the programs they offer.

As part of the initiative, together these schools were required to raise an additional $3.46 million as a match to the Lila Wallace-Reader's Digest Fund grants. The money, along with the balance of the Fund's award, would be used to create or augment permanent endowments to ensure the long-term vitality of the schools.

In December 1991, Carl Atkins wrote a memo to all Guild members:

It is my understanding that the Lila Wallace-Reader's [Digest] Fund will consider establishing other rounds of grants after a review and evaluation of the initial proposals. Your colleagues in the selected institutions carry a heavy responsibility because they are virtually acting as the vanguard for the field as a whole. I know you will rejoice in their good fortune and, at the same time, join with me in wishing them well. Their success will bode well for you and for all other schools in the Guild.

By the end of the grant period six years later, 167 member schools had participated in the program. Most received financial assistance, made possible through the generous support of the Lila Wallace-Reader's Digest Fund, which had awarded $1.2 million to the National Guild and $7 million in direct grants to community schools.

The National Guild and its member schools, and indeed the field as a whole, owes the Fund, its Board and staff, and the members of the Study team a profound debt of gratitude for literally putting community schools of the arts on the map. As the Fund had hoped, their generous support gave the Guild genuine credibility, national name recognition, and an entrée into sources of program funding from other major foundations. There was no way we could express our appreciation except to recognize and thank them publicly.

So in November 2005, at the national conference in Pittsburgh, the National Guild presented its Leadership Award (formerly the Colonel Samuel Rosenbaum Memorial Award) to the Wallace Funds.[15] The ceremony was attended by a large audience consisting of community school directors, staff, trustees, and invited guests who joined with the Guild in enthusiastic applause. The award was accepted on behalf of the Funds by Rory Macpherson.

Chapter Fourteen
Sea Change

Why stay we on earth unless to grow?

– Robert Browning[1]

There was wide-spread acclamation in response to the Lila Wallace-Reader's Digest Fund's extraordinary recognition of the Guild. Their grants to the field of community arts schools and to the Guild gave us all a level of credibility never experienced before. With that, the Guild's relationship with its own members as well as its standing as the representative for the field changed irrevocably. At a meeting with Rory MacPherson and Joy Marie Abulokwe (staff members at the LilaWallace-Reader's Fund), Lolita Mayadas was told that the Fund was committed to a long-term relationship with the Guild and the schools.[2] She was also told that the Fund had a tradition of employing national service organizations in a re-granting role. The Guild was fortunate to be accepted as a trusted partner in that capacity. Better yet, other major grant makers soon began to follow the Fund's example.

To top it off, Jessica Chao issued an invitation[3] to 104 individuals representing national and New York City-based foundations, corporations, and federal agencies to a meeting on July 9, 1992, at which the results of the Fund's study of community arts schools were presented. Copies of the Report and the Executive Summary were also distributed, thus making them available to a broader audience of decision makers.

We were experiencing growth in all directions. It had been just a decade since Azim Mayadas had been placed in charge of membership development. In those ten years, the number of members had grown from 100 to 220. The Guild was becoming more comfortable in its own skin, with a vastly increased budget, expanding membership, and growing support from a host of new funders. In addition, we were providing leadership by identifying model programs at the local level and replicating them through re-granting programs and dissemination of information.

The Guild was also becoming more visible and its presence "at the table" more frequent and meaningful. In June 1992, we were invited to give a presentation at the Overview Panel for the National Endowment for the Arts Advancement Program. That same year, the National Endowment for the Arts, the National Endowment for the Humanities, and the U.S. Department of Education jointly funded an Arts Education Partnership Working Group. Approximately 47 artists and educators were invited to meet and make recommendations for the Secretary of Education, with James D. Wolfensohn, Chair of the Kennedy Center for the Performing Arts, moderating the session. Lolita Mayadas was asked to serve on a subcommittee that was charged with designing a national arts education dissemination center.

The Guild was changing from a small service organization into an association with the power of the purse and a voice that was becoming stronger and more relevant by the day. However, the change was not universally welcomed because of the perception that the association was turning into a threat, colorfully described by Trustee Janet Hunt as "the 800-pound gorilla" in the room. Some schools stridently complained that the Guild was raising money in competition with its own members, thereby reducing the funds available to the field. In point of fact, the Guild tried (with one or two known exceptions) to avoid approaching funders which supported, or might support, the schools directly. The goal was always to design programs that would benefit member schools as a whole and to seek grants from large, national funders which would be unlikely to support smaller institutions. As Board Chair, Carl Atkins pointed out in his December 1991 letter to members, "Almost 90% of all grant monies [will] go right back in program related financial support and services."

In spite of these efforts, however, it was difficult for every member to become accustomed to the Guild's new profile, especially in the New York area where chapter schools arranged a meeting to air their grievances. The atmosphere was testy to say the least. Members of the Board and management who were present tried to assuage the concerns of the schools, but there was little they could do in the practical sense except to offer assurances that they would try to avoid potential conflicts in future, especially with new funders. However, some members remained unconvinced and immediately after the meeting, the 92nd Street Y School of Music, Greenwich House Music School, and three or four others left the Guild, an outcome we deeply regretted. Nevertheless, it made absolutely no strategic sense to go back to the "old" Guild. The organization was on a path forward, and it was neither feasible nor desirable to reverse course.

With such profound changes taking place all at once, there were bound to be growing pains and challenges that would need to be addressed. Realizing this, the Executive Committee of the Board began to work on key elements of a Long-Range Plan at its meeting in November 1992 that focused squarely on strengthening the Guild's financial resources and the role of the Board as a whole. The meeting was an outcome of the Guild's second Board Retreat, which had been held nine months earlier and led by Halsey and Alice North. The current Retreat provided an opportunity for the Board to:

- Examine the Guild's history (particularly its rapid growth during the 1980's)

- Discuss the impact of the field's expansion

- Consider the opportunities presented by the Lila Wallace-Reader's Digest Fund grant for the *GuildTech* program

- Begin developing a Long-Range Plan

By October 1992 the Guild had successfully drafted a three-year long-range plan, which laid out the primary challenges facing the organization: first, to develop greater institutional strength and stability, and second, to ensure that the Guild [would be] equal to the expectations it [had] created.[4] The Executive Summary included the following paragraph:

"In developing goals and objectives, the mission of the Guild and its service orientation were always uppermost: Whom do we serve? What do we do? Why should we do it? On the assumption that the answers lie in the nature of the programs the Guild offers to its membership, it soon becomes obvious that program goals must serve as the driving force behind the entire long-range plan."

The overall goals were spelled out as follows:

- To stabilize the programs and services of the Guild

- To stabilize the Guild's operations

- To leverage greater support for member schools

- To make the Guild recognizable as the voice of the movement

- To make the Guild indispensable in the lives of its schools

The Guild also began to discuss the feasibility of a national capital campaign aided by Willem Brans and Steven J. Bronfenbrenner from the C.W. Shaver Company.[5] The campaign had two objectives: first, to raise funds from national funders for the purpose of re-granting monies to small and medium-sized community schools, and second, to establish a general endowment fund to support Guild's general operations. A detailed case statement for what was called the National Community Arts Fund was published in the spring of 1994 with a three-year campaign goal of $2.25 million to support community initiatives, technical assistance and training, and the establishment of cash reserve and endowment funds. To aid that effort, a Leadership Council for the National Community Arts Fund was formed in 1994 with Don V. Seibert, former Chairman of J.C. Penney, Inc., as Chair and Grant Beglarian, former Dean of Performing Arts at the University of Southern California, as Advisor. Both individuals were members of the Guild's Board of Trustees.

For reasons that are not entirely clear, little came of this effort and the campaign was suspended in 1995.[6] A statement dated June 1,

1996, shows an invested endowment fund of $146,000 yielding $8,200 in annual income.

In terms of annual contributed income, there was a considerable increase in the number of funders and the size of grants. By November 11, 1992, the Guild had received $55,000 in unrestricted grants, thereby exceeding the budgeted total by $10,000, plus $126,850 in restricted grants for programs. The budgeted target for unrestricted corporate and foundation grants was $45,000, a far cry from $26,500 just two years earlier. It was encouraging that the Guild had been successful in attracting the support of seven new grant makers. Further, two additional funders returned after a hiatus of 3-4 years.

The Guild had also been successful in regaining the interest of the Josephine Bay Paul and C. Michael Paul Foundation for Repro, a pilot program to replicate model public school/community school partnerships for which the Foundation had approved a 3-year grant of $92,350 in 1992. A sum of $5,000 was also made available under the new grant to enable the Guild to hire a part-time project director one day per week for 50 weeks. It should be remembered that the Foundation (now renamed Bay and Paul Foundations) had given the Guild its first major grant of $10,000 for general support way back in 1983, and they continued to provide generous support over the years through the intercession of its Program Director, Dianne Daniels. The last grant the Guild received from them was for the Partners in Excellence Program in 2000.

To cope with the extra responsibilities incurred by new programs, the Guild urgently needed additional staff. And by April 1995 the following three new full-time staff members were in place: Jonathan Herman, Director of Training; Alison Rubin, Development Associate; and Lois Hubbard, Bookkeeper/Office Assistant. Job responsibilities for existing staff were also changed. Azim Mayadas, Managing Director, was made responsible for operations, financial oversight, membership recruitment and certification, and the New Arts Schools and Centers (NASCENT) Program. Kate Brackett, Executive Assistant, was moved into a new Program Associate position with responsibility for tracking the Guild's grant programs as well as conference/seminar registration and logistics.

Jonathan Herman was later named Executive Director of the Guild, two years after my retirement. He turned out to be a great asset to the Guild. Initially, he was interested in applying for the Director of Development position, but I felt that his background perfectly suited him to be Program Director and he accepted the job. Jonathan was formerly the Program Director at New York's Rhinelander Center, where he was responsible for the administration and operation of the Early Childhood, After School Visual and Performing Arts, Parenting, and Deaf and Hard of Hearing Programs. He had a Master's degree in Education from Teacher's College, Columbia University with a concentration in communication, computing, and technology in education. In his capacity as the Guild's Program Director, his responsibilities included marketing and administration of technical assistance programs, annual seminars, and the national conference.

Jonathan possessed a sunny, optimistic temperament, and he was easy to get along with. He was particularly skilled at the implementation of programs and thoroughly detail-oriented. Perhaps his greatest asset was that he was able to build consensus even when issues were contentious. He also had a knack for small talk in social situations and was always in touch with the latest news and views (as well as gossip!)

More importantly, his exemplary staff work was an essential factor in the successful execution of seminal programs such as Partners in Excellence and Creative Communities. Also, because of his background in education, he was in tune with the changing perspectives of educators, federal priorities such as Goals 2000, and the needs of funders. He helped develop highly professional evaluations of the Guild's major initiatives – an invaluable resource for all concerned. And he also enabled community arts schools and their public school partners to understand and replicate best practices by disseminating information broadly through reports and seminars.

Aside from the Guild's success in terms of grants and membership growth, we were also expanding into new ground in other areas. It was a time when the Internet was just coming into general use. Jeffrey Bezos had founded Amazon in 1995, and e-commerce seemed a viable option for business purposes. Azim began to explore the idea of creating a website for the Guild and it was launched in 1997. The site was also painstakingly placed on over 200 search engines. The Guild was probably among the first arts associations in the country to have its own website and to offer the ability to purchase materials on line. That project also evolved into a valuable membership benefit since full-page descriptions were created for each member school and uploaded on the site. Links to schools that already had their own pages were also posted. We learned later that the website had 60,000 successful hits following its placement on the Internet in April. This included hits to any file on the site, including 40 member-school extension pages.

During one week alone in mid-September, there were over 5,000 hits.[7]

In order to offer greater opportunities for feedback from member schools, a Council of School Directors was established November 1995. This Council consisted of a body of 33 Guild school directors expressly constituted to advise the Board and staff on policy, programs, and planning. The goal was for the Council to reflect the geographic diversity of the Guild. Thus, each chapter was represented by its Chapter Chair plus additional elected members, or approximately one director for every ten schools in that chapter.

The six-year period from 1991 through 1996 was perhaps the most momentous in the Guild's long history. One of the highlights during that time was the second National Festival of the Arts with President and Mrs. Clinton as Honorary Co-Chairs. The event was held in November 1994 at the Kennedy Center for the Performing Arts, Washington D.C. The Guild was charged no rental fees due to the extraordinary generosity of its Chairman, James Wolfensohn. Modeled on the earlier Carnegie Hall Festival, the event included a performance by a new National Youth Orchestra with 93 players, conducted by Lukas Foss with violinist, Elmar Oliveira as soloist. In addition, there were also performances by a 99-member Youth Choir conducted by Henry Leck, a 21-member Youth Jazz Band led by Denis DiBlasio, a Performathon with 325 participants, and an Art Exhibit presenting 72 works by 28 children. Altogether, 565 students from all over the country participated in this series of events.

In terms of fundraising, a Development Report dated November 11, 1994, showed a healthy contributed income picture with $31,500 in unrestricted grants and major multi-year restricted grants for programs.[8]

And then, to cap it all off, there was cause for great excitement with the news that the Guild had received its first-ever Challenge Grant from the National Endowment for the Arts for $150,000 to support the Arts Access Program in 1995. It was an especially significant achievement given the stiff competition for Challenge Grants. Nearly 170 applications were received by the NEA that year for grants totaling close to $60 million. Of these, just 44 awards were approved, ranging from $75,000-$600,000. The Guild's application was funded in full.

The Arts Access Program consisted of two components:

- New Arts Schools and Centers (NASCENT), which provided seed grants, management training, and technical assistance to approximately 24 underserved communities to start new community schools, and

- Community Partnership Action (COMPACT), a new initiative that awarded grants to community schools to expand their financial aid programs.

Both components were intended to encourage significant community input and participation at each school site.

In sailing parlance, the weather was set to fair. The wind was at our backs, skies were blue, and waters calm. But, beyond the horizon a storm was brewing that turned out to be as destructive as it was unexpected. And to this day, no one can explain what caused it.

Chapter Fifteen
Darkness at Noon[1]

Things are going to get a lot worse before they get worse.

– Lily Tomlin

The Guild's optimistic predictions of good times ahead overlooked worries that had surfaced for more than two decades about the Board's inability to raise funds. It was a recurring concern expressed by several previous executive directors, and the current Executive Director was no exception.

Be that as it may, matters came to a head in 1994 possibly because the stakes were significantly higher. Although approval for a second grant of $650,000 had been received from the Lila Wallace-Reader's Digest Fund for *GuildTech II* (starting in January 1995), no further grants from that source could be expected. The loss of such a significant source of income was potentially critical. But Board members, with some notable exceptions, seemed uncertain about what to do. An actionable strategy was urgently needed. Most of all, somebody in a leadership position needed to take hold of the reins.

In hopes of jump-starting the process, I set up a meeting with three of the Guild's office bearers (Carl Atkins, Robert Capanna, and Janet Hunt) on May 23, 1994, to discuss Board development and responsibilities. Regrettably, the meeting ended in failure and a total absence of common ground. It got to the point of such frustration that I lost my composure and had to leave the room temporarily. I was stressed out and desperate for

131

*money and support, but what I got was the shock of
disillusion. For me, the primary issue was whether the
Board was prepared to take hold of its fiduciary
responsibility to raise money or whether it would expect
me do that job virtually on my own, as before. I had hoped
for a productive discussion, but Bob Capanna pushed back
aggressively, implying that nothing was likely to change.
His retreat was a startling turn-around from his earlier
positions when he could be counted on to motivate the
Board and to support big, bold programs such as
NASCENT and the Carnegie Hall event. Yet on this
occasion, all he could say was that the Guild was doing
too much given scarce resources, which, to my mind,
somewhat begged the question.*

The day after the meeting, Lolita wrote a letter to Carl, Bob, and
Janet. Excerpts follow:

First of all, I want to thank you for taking the time to meet
with me yesterday. All in all, I felt it was a valuable
opportunity to talk about some things which really needed
to be addressed though I regret I allowed my emotions to
get the better of me....

I agree that we need to do a better job of motivating the
Board, and with communications, monitoring, follow-up,
and evaluation. Also, perhaps we can take less time on
committee reports at Board meetings and begin to address
real issues, tasks, problems, and challenges....At the same
time, it is crucial that the Board takes hold of its "donor,
door-opener" role. We should be concerned that a majority
do not, will not, or cannot, accept this. If Trustees are to be
exempted from this key responsibility, there should be
some very good reason why they [are] on the Board at all
(i.e. special skills, artistic achievement, etc.).... We must
make a strong effort to recruit committed people who have
influence and wealth. Many people in this peer group
understand that they will be asked to open doors....I do not
accept the view that these kinds of Board members are

difficult to get. We have a number of promising candidates and prospects. The challenge is to keep them once we [have] them....

We were fortunate that the Lila Wallace-Reader's Digest grant for *GuildTech II* had been renewed, thereby handing us a temporary reprieve. For a while, the situation seemed to improve, but the old contentious issues were still bubbling just beneath the surface.

Despite that, we began 1997 on a high note with elaborate plans to celebrate the Guild's 60th Anniversary in Philadelphia at the November conference together with the third National Festival of the Arts at the Academy of Music. On this occasion, the National Youth Orchestra was conducted by Leonard Slatkin, the Children's Choir by Henry Leck, and the Jazz Band by Jimmy Heath. There were 171 students in the Performathon and 57 students submitting 63 works of art for the Art Exhibit. Altogether, 69 schools participated in the event which was a strong artistic success. The Committee Chairs were Linda Shapiro and Carole Haas, each of whom generously donated $25,000 to support the event.

Bob Capanna had offered to raise a significant amount of money for the Festival, but he fell far short of his target. I believe he badly miscalculated his ability to meet his goals. He was a fundraiser without equal when soliciting funds for his own school. He also had some success raising funds for Guild programs from Philadelphia-based foundations. But to my mind, he was unable to grasp the difference between fundraising for a local, as against a national, organization.

His disappointment was obvious – in fact, at one point he was quoted as saying, "If I can't raise money, no one can." True or not, his failure represented a loss of face for him, and I believe that colored all his interactions with the Guild going forward.

Aside from that, a complicating factor was that I had not had time to prepare a budget for the following year prior to the November Board meeting, mostly because of the extra work load for the National Festival. I mentioned my lapse to the Guild's Treasurer, Arthur Judson, who took it equably, but when Bob was told of it, he was furious and took me severely to task. I had been derelict, but I remember thinking that his reaction was way out of proportion to the "crime" especially since this was the first time it had ever occurred.

A note from Lolita to Bob that spring about the 1998-1999 Strategic Plan, copied to the Executive Committee,[2] once again references the issue of Trustee responsibilities and participation.

Background

The tension over the lack of a budget is a symptom of a much greater anxiety about how the Guild will be financed in the post-Lila Wallace era. In this instance, history repeats itself.

You will recall the meeting I had with you, Carl Atkins, and Janet Hunt in 1994 coming up to the end of the first Lila Wallace-Reader's Digest grant. The question then is the same as now – after Lila Wallace, what?....The major burden of responsibility then, as now, rested squarely on the Executive Director....This structural dependence on one individual is both unwise and untenable. I would assume that the Board shares this view.

So now, three years later, here we are facing exactly the same situation. Why? Because we have failed to address the single, critical issue of the Board's responsibility for fundraising. Though the responsibility is accepted in principle, it is not carried out in practice.

Regardless of how much, or how little, the Guild does and how much we bring in from earned revenues, the bottom line is that we must raise money.

After the Festival was over, I was summoned to the Settlement Music School in Philadelphia to meet with Bob on January 16, 1998.

As far as I recall, I was not told David Lapin and Janet Hunt (Board President and Vice Chair respectively) would also be there. The stated purpose was to discuss the outlines of a new budget for 1998. I recall Bob sitting at a small table against the wall, facing me. His attitude was hostile and confrontational. He insisted that it was not sustainable for the Guild to continue raising funds based on its current program-based strategies. I demurred and pointed out that the only way for us to raise major amounts of money was through grants for programs. As Carl Shaver had declared to the Board as far back as November 1973, "Funds for a national office are difficult to raise and ... attention should be focused on expansion and program development." Regardless, Bob was adamant about changing that model and asked for three-year draft budget projections based on three alternative scenarios, as described below:

> Scenario A was predicated on the Guild being able to raise $250,000/year for technical assistance, which would throw off administrative overhead based on current practices. Scenario B was a scaled back version... that included project funds already secured but with less optimistic projections for major new project support. Scenario C was a bare-bones budget that included project funds already secured but anticipated no new project support.[3]

The day after the meeting on January 17, 1998, Bob circulated a memo to all present. Two passages from that memo stand out. First, Bob noted that David and he "recorded their lack of enthusiasm for Plan A and our assessment that it was not a feasible long-term strategy for the Guild." And second, he and David recorded their willingness to step down at any time going forward. "We agreed," he wrote, "that a consultative and cooperative relationship was a necessary pre-condition for our continuing in office." He and David also suggested that "Lolita might do better with Board leadership that shared her vision of the future for the Guild and with leadership with whom there was not an ongoing conflict." He also pointed out neither he nor David was committed to standing for a second term at the Annual Meeting in November.

All three scenarios, projected to FY 2000, were duly dispatched to members of the Executive Committee and a conference call took place on Monday, February 23, 1998.

It was obvious from these figures that Scenarios B and C were not sustainable.

Operating Funds FY 2000	Income	Expenses	Surplus (Loss)
Scenario A	$372,000	$372,000	-0-
Scenario B	$208,750	$343,000	($34,250)
Scenario C	$194,250	$202,000	($7,750)

During the call, Lolita Mayadas explained that the Guild would need to take in $32,000 for administrative overhead from new program grants in 1998. She also spelled out four reasons for raising program monies:

1) Demonstrated success

2) Substantial monies spun off for the Guild's operating funds (administrative overhead)

3) Support for programs by member schools

4) Ongoing interest by major funders

Bob Capanna expressed his concerns at this approach, pointing out that this strategy, taken forward into the next three years, would mean that the Guild would need to raise over $378,000 in restricted funds by the year 2000 in order to derive projected overhead from programs.

Although no formal vote was requested to approve the budget, committee members expressed their opinion as follows:

Arthur Judson, Treasurer of the Board, felt confident that the Scenario A budget was doable. He added that lower objectives were self-defeating and the Board would gravitate downward toward them. Janet Hunt also felt that the budget was workable. Alice Pfaelzer approved the budget and suggested that we review it again in three months. Lowell Noteboom approved it in principle but had some concerns about the need to raise substantial restricted grants on an ongoing basis. Robert Capanna did not approve the budget, noting that the Finance Committee would need to review it. That Committee duly considered it at their meeting on March 4 and approved the budget "contingent upon the development of Board strategies for raising contributed income." [4]

The above scenarios were presented by Lolita on March 7, 1998, at the Guild's next Board meeting. Andrew Silverstein, the Guild's accountant, presented the audited figures for the previous year. At the Board's request, he also presented an "environmental scan of non-profits." [5] The meeting produced more than its fair share of drama with Bob insisting that the Guild's current fundraising strategies were not sustainable. This view was challenged by several members of the Board as well as Andrew, who pointed out that the Guild's recent record proved otherwise. Much to Bob's annoyance, Andrew also remarked that the Board "seemed to have a real fear of success."[6] Bob pushed back, implying that Andrew was speaking out of turn. "Nobody asked you," he insisted. But Iona Benson, who was a lot tougher than she looked, and a generous donor, was having none of that. She stood up. "I asked him," she said firmly, putting an end to further argument.

Eventually, the Scenario A budget was approved but with a reduction of $32,500, which included $5,000 in staff salary increases. However, it was agreed that vigorous efforts would be taken by Board and staff to restore some, if not all, of these cuts.

As requested, Lolita then presented a statement of Trustee contributions for 1997. To summarize: twenty-five Trustees had contributed $25,000; twelve Trustees had not contributed anything; of these, three had made gifts for the 1997 Festival. A lengthy discussion then took place. Inevitably, as the person responsible for soliciting Trustee gifts, Bob Capanna took some heat for poor results. To his credit, however, he immediately offered to set up a subcommittee of the Development Committee to contact all Board members "in order to discuss their capability for personal giving as well as other ways they may be able to assist the Guild to raise needed funds."

On May 12, 1998, Bob wrote a note to the Board:

As you may recall, we agreed at our March meeting that Lowell Noteboom and I would form a small sub-committee to try and move our planning process to a conclusion. With Lolita, we arrived at a group that included Lowell, Carl Atkins, Angelica Berrie, Karen Romeo, Lydia Kontos, Linda Shapiro, Lolita and Jonathan from the staff, and me, ex- officio.

Lolita suggested that the work of this committee could benefit from professional guidance and suggested that we engage Sherry Schiller as facilitator. I was enthusiastic about her suggestion because of the very positive experience we had with Sherry at the Guild's Leadership Seminar of a year or so ago. Sherry brings a wealth of information and experience to our effort.

The small group met with Sherry in New York this past week and did important preliminary work on the plan that will form the basis of our conversation in June. As you know, Lowell cannot be with us then and Sherry has agreed to lead the session.

I want to thank you in advance for your patience and help with this process and to particularly recognize Lowell's extremely useful work that has lead [sic] us to this point.

The meeting on June 5 began well enough, but by the end it had turned into a disaster with accusations of sedition and conspiracy directed at me. Specifically, I was taken to task for lobbying to remove executive officers of the Board. I was speechless. I couldn't think what I had said or done to deserve these attacks. It is true that I had confided in Sherry about my disagreements with Bob and my unhappiness with his recent behavior. I thought it important she should know about the developing rift so she could find ways to address it in a professional manner in the context of the planning effort. But that did not happen. I remember being deeply disappointed. Anyhow, it was too late — the damage had been done. Later, it occurred to me that Bob may also have had private conversations with her. If that were true, she would have been in an ideal position to act as mediator.

The irony is that the Guild was continuing to secure major grants from various sources.[7] Thanks to Toby Mayman, a Guild Trustee, The Colburn Fund, endowed by its founder, Richard D. Colburn, approved a $150,000 grant for the NASCENT program. In addition, we received $150,000 from the Ahmanson Foundation also for NASCENT and $120,000 from the Open Society Institute for the Arts Access pilot program to provide arts instruction to children and youth in public housing. Other Board members were also involving themselves in the fundraising effort. All this represented a welcome ray of sunshine in an otherwise dismal year.

Another morale builder was that the Guild was nominated for the National Medal of the Arts, which is awarded by the President of the United States to individuals or groups who "...are deserving of special recognition by reason of their outstanding contributions to the excellence, growth, support and availability of the arts in the United States." In the end, the Guild was not chosen to receive the medal, but it was an honor to be considered.

Also, miraculously, there was a remarkable response from the Board in terms of personal contributions. Thanks to the efforts of the subcommittee (now consisting of Angelica Berrie, Bob Capanna, Lydia Kontos, and Kathy Schumacher) we had received $40,625 in cash and pledges with responses from six Trustees still due. Bob Capanna noted the major increase in Board giving and suggested that the Board needed to study the process in order to annualize this success. He also suggested the establishment of a group to cultivate and develop corporate and foundation gifts.[8]

Despite all those positive developments, the relationship between Lolita and Bob was going from bad to worse, and charges and counter-charges expressed in writing continued throughout the spring of 1998 culminating with the Board meeting on June 6.

The following brief summary of the Board's action on that day was sent to Lolita by Bob for insertion in the Minutes:

> The Board of Trustees went into executive session "to discuss the relationship of the executive director to the executive officers of the board.
>
> After discussion, it was moved and seconded:
>
> That a letter of reprimand to the executive director be drafted by the chairman for approval by the executive committee, that the letter, when sent, be copied to the board of trustees, and that the chairman and the president conduct a performance review of the executive director. Further, that the chairman report this motion to the executive director at the conclusion of this meeting.
>
> The motion passed with 13 in favor and 4 opposed; the chair did not vote."

Bob followed up with a letter to Lolita, dated June 11, and copied to the entire Board of Trustees. It is reproduced here in its entirety:

> The Board of Trustees of the Guild has directed me by a motion passed at their meeting of June 6, 1998 to write you this letter to express their concern about your recent unacceptable behavior toward and relationship with the executive officers of the Guild.
>
> Specifically, the board noted the inappropriateness of the tone and content of your letters to me in response to my letter of late November 7, 1997. Further, the board expressed displeasure with your efforts to subvert the roles of the elected leadership of the board by lobbying trustees for their removal from office and by convening ad hoc groups of trustees to consider issues that are properly of the purview of the executive officers, executive committee or other standing committees of the board.

The board has also directed the president and me to conduct a performance review of your work as executive director of the Guild in the near future.

You have expressed some confusion regarding the existing leadership structure of the board. The Committee on Trustees would welcome your suggestions or questions as to these roles as they relate to you.

On a personal note, I would urge you to be clear and direct in your communication with me and the other officers of the board and to bring to our attention any and all matters that you feel impede your effectiveness as executive director so that they can be resolved promptly.

The board desires and expects and I personally desire and expect a constructive and collaborative relationship with you going forward. I remain committed to working with you on behalf of the Guild as do the president and vice chairman.

A flurry of letters to Bob from several Board members followed. They were not requested by me, neither was I informed that they were being written until well after the fact when I received copies forwarded by several Trustees. I had been officially accused, in absentia, of subversion and conspiracy without any evidence. I was neither allowed to speak on my own behalf, nor was I permitted to enter a plea of any kind. I was indicted without benefit of due process and charged accordingly.

For the record, I now append pertinent extracts from three of those letters in the hope that they will serve as witness for my defense.

Iona Benson June 22, 1998

First, I feel that your letter does not fairly represent the Board and second...I find the tone of the letter so unnecessarily punitive that in my opinion we have lost the ground that all of us had been working toward.

The Board was called into Executive Session, and as such should have viewed your letter before it was sent out. This request was made, but in the last minute rush to push through a vote, it was ignored, and a move was made that only the Executive Committee should approve your draft of the letter. So to say that the Board "directed" you to "write you **this** letter" is untrue.

Further, [in your letter] to Lolita you quote the Board as noting "the inappropriateness of the tone and content of your letters to me in response to my letter of late November, 1997." Bob, you raised that question. You asked the Board if it did not agree with you that Lolita's response was "totally inappropriate." There were those who responded in the affirmative, but there were many of us who did not respond. I, for one, feel that her response to you was inevitable given the fact that she had been summoned to Philadelphia to appear before you and David and Janet and that that meeting was followed by more harsh correspondence, as though Lolita were in the habit of not submitting a budget on time.

No motion was passed on that. No vote was taken.

As for the rest of the letter, you quote the Board as "expressing displeasure" with various actions you attribute to Lolita: "convening ad hoc committees, etc." "efforts to subvert the roles of the elected leadership," and so on. You don't mention it in your letter but you went so far as to say that certain funders now refuse to speak to Lolita. This is all pretty powerful stuff. And it seems to reflect the difficulties between you and Lolita. Rather than say so, you have shifted all these complaints to the Board....

The very desire on your part to use the word "insubordination" chills my blood. To be insubordinate is "to be disobedient to the orders of superiors." I thought that all of us were peers, that all of us were working toward the same goals.

Disagreement is bound to occur in any organization. It is to be expected unless the organization be dead. But disagreement is not grounds for humiliation and reprimand.

Charles Farmer, July 6, 1998

Those not present at the meeting will not know that at the opening of the meeting, or soon after, you demanded that a letter of reprimand be sent to the Executive Director or we would have your and the President's resignation forthwith (clearly an ultimatum with which we were not comfortable)... I know that even for some who voted for the resolution there was discomfort with the lack of real "resolution" of the matter. After the majority vote in favor of a letter, it was requested that we all would have a chance to see a draft of the letter before it was sent, but that request was quashed, and it was quickly decided that the draft would be shown only to the Executive Committee before sending it.

In short, I do not view anything in her letters as rising to the level deserving of a written "reprimand."

As to the... "convening [of] ad hoc groups of trustees to consider issues that are properly the purview of the executive officers, executive committee or other standing committees of the board," I simply cannot recall anything from the June 6 meeting, other than perhaps a vague passing statement, that defined any such alleged impropriety. Perhaps some members of the board knew what was being referred to, but I daresay many, including myself, did not. No details were given, and certainly that issue was not debated.

Alice Pfaelzer, July 21, 1998

I was pleased to read the copy of your performance review of Lolita and hope that this will signal a better working relationship between Board officers and staff. I also want you to know that I thoroughly agree with everything that was said by Iona in her letter to you, and with what Charles put in his letter. Although I do not want to prolong a battle that has gone on too long, I do not want to remain an "innocent bystander."

In particular, I strongly agree with Charles that Lolita has done a remarkable job over the past 17 years in bringing the Guild from what it was when she began as Executive Director, to where it is today. I also want you to know that, although I have always had a wonderful, warm, and open relationship with her, she has never "lobbied" me for removal of any officer of the Board. She has always asked my advice as to how she could better work with the officers for the good of the organization, but there has never been even a hint that she wanted to start a movement to remove anyone from office.

Earlier in the year, Toby Mayman, the Executive Director of The Colburn School of Performing Arts, had also written to Bob expressing concerns by several Board members about "what seems the creation of a 'mini' executive committee within the executive committee consisting of you, [Bob], Janet Hunt and David." [9] Her concerns were echoed by Donna Merris, who deplored the formation of what she viewed as a "Troika."[10]

Meantime, the Strategic Planning Committee, headed by Lowell Noteboom, had been working diligently on a new draft document which was circulated for input and comment prior to the Board meeting in November. Bob was not impressed, as his letter below will show:

Bob Capanna to Executive Committee, October 27, 1998

At the risk of sounding churlish, I did want to briefly record my reaction to the Strategic Plan and other recent developments. Since I am the titular chair of the Guild, I did not want my silence interpreted as acquiescence. On the other hand, I am sick of broadside communications to the board, so I thought a memo to the executive committee would be a compromise way of going on record.

It is hard to argue with much of the plan, since it is largely a call to continue doing what the Guild has done. My concern is that it does not acknowledge that the Guild is in crisis and that some really new approaches might be called for.

My sense is that this crisis is both internal and external. We are aware of the disaffection of considerable numbers of "important" schools, the New York contingent being the most viable example. I have reported to you my concern that many of the directors I most respect take no active role (and are not encouraged to take a role) in the Guild. I would also submit that several of us who have taken active roles in the past will not do so in the future.

Suffice it to say that there was no meeting of minds and the rupture was irreparable.

Chapter Sixteen
Aftermath

"Tut, Tut, child," said the Duchess, *"there's a moral in everything if only you can find it."*

– Lewis Carroll[1]

The Guild could not continue in this current state of tension forever. Something had to give. The first moves were made by Bob Capanna and David Lapin, who decided that they did not wish to stand for re-election. Their letters were both dated July 23, 1998, prior to Bob's October 27th letter expressing dissatisfaction with the strategic plan.

<u>Bob Capanna to Janet Hunt</u>

My conflict has been in trying to weigh my chances of being effective as chairman against the personal cost of the job to me in terms of time, energy and satisfaction.

My evaluation has been colored by my assessment of my past effectiveness. I do not believe that I have succeeded in leading the board to consensus on many of the issues we have faced. In particular, I regret that I have been unable to persuade the board that the root of the recent conflicts with Lolita and, perhaps, among board members, is other than a clash of personalities. While I am convinced that it is not so, others clearly are not.

Further, I do not see that things will be substantially different going forward. Since none of the basic dynamics have changed, I believe that future conflicts, when and if

147

they arise, will also be characterized as personal in nature. In retrospect, there is a long history of this in the culture of the Guild.

I have therefore concluded that it would be in the best interests of all concerned if I did not stand for a second term as chairman or as trustee of the Guild.

David Lapin to Janet Hunt

I have decided not to run for re-election as president of the National Guild in November. Nor do I wish to continue to serve on the Board.

Returning from vacation this week, I discover that some Board members still wish to continue a debate which was resolved by a Board vote in June. I do not believe that the Board can operate effectively in this climate. I am certain that Board officers cannot operate effectively in this climate, and for this reason I will end my presidency in November.

I wish to take this opportunity to thank you and Bob Capanna for giving so much of yourselves in the service of the Guild. Perhaps our successors will find a way to eliminate the endless bickering and second guessing which have so eroded my commitment to a thankless role. For the Guild's sake, I certainly hope so.

The controversy was put to rest at the Annual Meeting on November 14, 1998, when Board member, Lydia Kontos was called upon to address the membership in the absence of the Chairman [Bob Capanna], Vice-Chairman [Janet Hunt] and President [David Lapin]. Her presentation was well reasoned, dispassionate, and pitch-perfect as the following excerpt from the Minutes will show:

Noting that questions and rumors had been circulating among some members, Ms. Kontos said she would prefer to address the issue directly and candidly. To begin with, she pointed out that none of the three officers had resigned per se. Rather, they had decided not to stand for re-election. Second, she noted that Janet Hunt had informed the Board early in the year that because of other growing commitments she would not stand for re-election and further, that she could not attend the conference.

Ms. Kontos recognized that there had been conflicts. In such a situation, she said, one of two things happen: people stay and resolve them, or they leave, which is what the Chairman and President decided to do. As far as their absence at the conference was concerned she noted that the decision had been made by them on an individual basis. She closed by remarking that the leadership is not entrenched and that there should be no automatic expectation of re-election on the part of any trustee or officer of the Board.

She asked if there were any questions from the floor about this issue. There being none, she concluded her report and comments.

Lydia Kontos had served the Guild for many years as a Board member and in various officer positions. In her professional capacity, she was Executive Director of the Elaine Kauffman Cultural Center in New York – and one of the most effective and successful executives in the Guild's constituency. In personal terms, she was endowed with great charm, shrewd intelligence, and unerring political skills. She also possessed an infectious sense of humor which helped to defuse tense situations. I had the greatest respect for her and sometimes sought her out for advice, which she always gave me honestly and tactfully. She was a model Trustee, always ready to help out in whatever capacity she was needed. It was fortunate that it fell to her as Board Secretary and a member of the Governance Committee to present the report of that Committee at the Annual Meeting, a responsibility she handled with

*customary professionalism and candor without
taking sides or casting blame.*

There was a palpable sense of relief when it was all over, but the battle had neither been lost nor won. Inevitably, it took some time for the organization to recover from its self-inflicted trauma. The entire episode had played out over conflicting visions for the Guild. On his side, Bob was unhappy with the path chosen and roundly criticized it at every opportunity throughout 1998.

Yet to this day, I am at a loss as to what he wanted us to do. He objected to almost every aspect of "my" vision, but, to my knowledge, no ideas (however sketchy) emerged from his side except for three budget scenarios. The only clue was his written comment on October 27, 1998, that "some really new approaches might be called for." Since he did not define what that meant, no discussions took place and no alternative vision was ever addressed at Board level.

Aside from that, I deeply regret the breakdown of a partnership that was behind some of the Guild's greatest achievements. There are two sides to every question and I must accept some of the blame for Bob's grievances. But I still I do not understand why it all changed so abruptly.

Bob passed away in 2018 at age 65 after a long illness. We never made up our quarrel. Obviously, he is unable to comment on this chapter. Although I have tried to present his side of the story fairly, based on his communications with me and others, I recognize that this approach could be interpreted as one-sided and incomplete. I therefore turned to David Lapin in August 2019 to ask for his reading of the situation. His response follows in its entirety:

David Lapin to Lolita Mayadas, via email, August 7, 2019

The causes of the "rupture" were structural and personal. With respect to the former, the Guild in those days really had little infrastructure in place to run a conference and a festival of the arts. As a result, you needed to draw greatly on the resources of area schools, and Bob was feeling pressure from his staff that the "draw" was excessive. As I recall, the breaking point came over repertoire for the orchestra which in Bob's mind had been settled upon by him and Leonard Slatkin. I think you had made some suggestion for change, perhaps eliminating *Estancia* for a more popular repertoire choice, and he basically lost it. You can correct me on this if you recall it differently.

The second structural problem flowed from the Guild's lack of a written succession plan, which put you, me and Bob at a disadvantage not knowing precisely how and when you might retire, although I do recall that the three of us had some conversations on this subject, prior to the Philadelphia conference. All of this contributed to an atmosphere of uncertainty, which was aggravated by the personal issues.

Once Bob got it into his head that the two of you were not working well together, he had set upon a course that ultimately resulted in his resignation. I think in retrospect he just could not let go and move on, as I did when we effectively reconciled in Boulder two years later. It's all water under the bridge at this point... By the way, the impetus for my resignation came from Charles Farmer, who also couldn't move on and unintentionally fueled the flames at the next board meeting post Philadelphia. I had it at that point and decided the honorable thing to do was resign.... I attribute this decision to the indiscretions of youth, and would have handled it differently had I a few more years of patience and maturity under my belt.

Bottom line: you and Azim did more for the field than anyone else and the unfortunate incident pales in comparison to your joint accomplishments.

Chapter Seventeen
Creative Communities

*listen: there's a hell of a good universe next door;
let's go.*

— e.e.cummings

After an abysmal year, it was a relief to return to business that was, if anything, better than usual, with many positive developments.[1] Some highlights during 1998-2000 were:

Under the leadership of Lowell Noteboom, Chairman of the Planning Committee, the Arts for All Strategic Plan 1999-2003 brochure was published.

There were four focal points:

- Advocacy. We will become a significant national voice on behalf of the community arts school movement. That will include developing a clear message which can be effectively communicated to both internal and external constituencies.

- Membership. We will retain the members we have and take steps to grow the membership, including bringing into the Guild substantially all of the eligible community arts education organizations in the country.

- Programming Support to the Field. We will provide to the best of our ability programmatic support to Guild members that responds to their identified needs and preferences.

- Financial Stability. We will build the capacity and infrastructure of the Guild by developing the resources needed to support our mission.

In essence, the strategic plan launched a process through which diverse organizations, sharing similar goals, work together *to ensure that all Americans appreciate and understand the value of the arts in their own lives and in the life of their communities*. That statement was adopted as the Guild's mission.

- Katherine Schumacher, an active and long-time Trustee, was elected Chairman of the Board in 1998.

- Contributions from the Board had increased to just over $59,000 with 100% participation. Two categories for Board members were introduced: $1,000 for school directors and $5,000 for lay members.

- 51 new institutional members joined the Guild in 1999 and 2000.

- The Guild received a number of generous grants, including:

  - $100,000 for the Partners in Excellence Project from the Josephine Bay Paul and C. Michael Paul Foundation.

  - A two-year grant of $50,000 from the William Randolph Hearst Foundation for general operating support.

  - $37,500 for AMICI 2000 from the Southwest Fund for Arts Education.

- Jonathan Herman was promoted to the position of Associate Director in February 1999.

- A Board Retreat was held under the guidance of David Bury and Associates in March 3, 2000.

- As of March 1, 2001, multi-year grants and contributions from all federal, foundation, and individual sources totaled $1,374,947.

At the Annual Meeting on November 11, 2000, Lolita Mayadas highlighted some of the Guild's main programmatic activities during the year, including the Arts Management in Community Institutions (AMICI) Seminar and Partners in Excellence. She also described the new Creative Communities Initiative (CCI), which supported free sequential arts instruction by community school faculty to children and youth living in public housing. Creative Communities had come about as the result of a three-year pilot program supported by a grant of $120,000 from the Open Society Institute and a one-year planning grant of $25,000 from NEA.

This Initiative represented the first-ever partnership between the U.S. Department of Housing and Urban Development (HUD), the National Endowment for the Arts (NEA), and the National Guild. It was launched in October 2000 as NEA's inaugural Challenge America Initiative – a great honor. Lolita explained that in the spring of 2000 the Guild secured a commitment of $3 million from HUD, which transferred these funds to NEA. In turn, NEA added a $500,000 contribution, making a total of $3.5 million for the full program. Added to that would be $500,000 from the Guild in matching funds. This was a seminal national program – the first of its kind – and it generated great media attention and the interest of several major funders, as will be seen below.

The Guild wasted no time basking in the extra exposure but set about looking for someone to head the project. After a nationwide search, Shawn Dove was appointed Project Director of CCI. His responsibilities included management of the project, liaison with all the partners and preparation of materials for the review panel, and publications. An imposing African American figure, Shawn was ideally suited for the job both in terms of temperament as well as experience. Prior to his appointment, he was a pioneering leader of the nation's Beacon School movement, serving as Program Director of one of New York City's first Beacon Schools, the Countee Cullen Community Center in Central Harlem, operated by the Harlem Children's Zone, Inc. During his decade of service at the Harlem Children's Zone, he was also the founding editor-in-chief of Harlem Overheard, an award-winning youth-produced newspaper, and spearheaded the recruitment and training of a team of adolescents who launched the Harlem Children's Zone Fitness & Nutrition Center. Shawn's qualifications included an undergraduate degree in English from Wesleyan University. He was also a graduate of Columbia University Business School's Institute for Not-for-Profit Management and a 1994 recipient of the Charles H. Revson Fellowship at Columbia University.

Much to the excitement of all concerned, a press release was issued in November 2000. The heading and first paragraph follow:

NATIONAL ENDOWMENT FOR THE ARTS

NEWS

For Immediate Release:
November 9, 2000

Contacts:
NEA: Katherine Wood   202-682-5570
HUD: Donna White   202-708-0685
NGCSA: Shawn Dove   201-871-3337

NEA, HUD AND NGCSA ANNOUNCE $4 MILLION INITIATIVE TO BRING ARTS TO YOUTH IN PUBLIC HOUSING

Washington, D.C.--The National Endowment for the Arts (NEA), the U.S. Department of Housing and Urban Development (HUD) and the National Guild of Community Schools of the Arts (NGCSA) today jointly announced plans to teach children and youth who live in public housing about the arts. The new grant initiative, called **Creative Communities**, will provide to youngsters free, weekly arts instruction by professional artists. Activities may range from early childhood arts programs to intensive instruction for youth who show particular talent.

Commenting on the program, Bill Ivey, NEA Chairman, wrote:

"Young people, particularly those at risk, can derive significant benefits from involvement in arts learning programs like this one. They can increase their self-esteem, improve their ability to communicate, develop their creativity and learn valuable job skills. We're excited about the value of this partnership and believe that together, we will be able to make important contributions on both the local and national level."

A second comment was provided by Lolita Mayadas, National Guild Executive Director:

> "This project reaches out to youngsters in communities at risk. It gives them a chance to read poetry, to play an instrument, to paint or to dance so that they might learn to be creative and to find creative solutions for themselves and the communities in which they live. This is about more than community revitalization – it's the revitalization of the human spirit. We look forward to working with HUD and NEA in carrying out this unique and exciting project."

By the end of 2001, much to everyone's delight (and perhaps surprise) the Guild had succeeded in raising $350,000 towards its required $500,000 match for CCI from the following funders plus several others which subsequently granted matching funds: [2]

Annenberg Foundation	$100,000
Arthur M. Blank Foundation	$ 75,000
Andrew W. Mellon Foundation	$ 50,000
Open Society Institute	$ 50,000
Ahmanson Foundation	$ 25,000
Horace Goldsmith Foundation	$ 25,000

Under a cooperative agreement with NEA, the Guild received $800,000, which it was expected to match with $500,000 from non-federal sources. It all looked great on paper, but a lot of things had to happen before the program could be launched.

And here is the story of how it all came together, up to the nail-biting conclusion, drawn from contemporaneous notes and emails. [Note: since there are two individuals with the same first name, Jonathan Herman is identified by his first name only while all references to Jonathan Katz include his first and last name.]

November 1997 – Leon Botstein, President of Bard College and Principal Conductor of the American Symphony Orchestra, gives the keynote address at the Guild's Philadelphia conference. He is also a member of the Board at the Open Society Institute. After his speech he meets up with Jonathan Herman and wants to know what we could do with a grant of $100,000.

Mid-1998 – Several service organizations, including the National Guild, are invited to comment on the NEA's new Challenge America Initiative, which is designed to strengthen families, communities, and our nation through the arts. The Initiative also emphasizes programs for at-risk youth.

Late-1998 – The Guild receives $120,000 from the Open Society Institute for a pilot program offering arts instruction to children and youth in public housing at three sites: Portland, Maine; Knoxville, Tennessee; and Philadelphia, Pennsylvania. The program is evaluated by Bruce Jones, Director, Consortium for Educational Policy Analysis, University of Missouri.

March 19, 1999 – Lolita and Guild Board member Bill Reeder meet with Scott Shanklin- Peterson, NEA's Senior Deputy Chairman about a possible national initiative to reach children and youth at risk. The Guild offers itself as a resource. Scott expresses interest. She suggests a grant of $25,000 for a planning effort.

November 1999 – Gloria Cousar, Assistant Deputy Secretary, Office of Public and Indian Housing, US Department of Housing and Urban Development, participates in a special panel on Federal Partnerships at the Guild's Conference in Boulder, Colorado. After the panel discussion Jonathan walks with her out of the hotel. She suggests a follow-up conversation.

March 2000 – A conference call takes place with Gloria Cousar, Lolita, and Jonathan. Lolita makes the case for programs for underserved youth in public housing communities in the context of the pilot program. She quotes statistics, highlighting the fact that 20% of residents in public housing are under 17 years of age. She also points to a developing trend where Guild schools are offering early childhood and after school arts classes at or near housing communities. The focus of any new program would be to improve the environment (quality of life) for the place that kids call home. Minutes before the call ends, Gloria tosses out a figure of $3 million, which was unheard of in the Guild's annals! Jonathan and Lolita can barely believe their ears...

March 22, 2000 – Jonathan attends a Public Consultation meeting at HUD.

May 3, 2000 – A meeting takes place at NEA with Scott Shanklin-Peterson and other high-level NEA officers.[3] Also present are Jonathan Katz, CEO of the National Assembly of State Arts Agencies, Bill Reeder, Lolita, and Jonathan.

May 10, 2000 – A high-level Planning Committee meets at the NEA[4] to help shape a national leadership initiative to provide arts instruction for children and youth in low income housing communities, based on existing models. Lolita and Jonathan are in attendance. The facilitator is Jonathan Katz.

May 23, 2000 – A conference call takes place with Gloria, Lolita, and Jonathan. Lolita seeks advice about how the Guild might strengthen arts programs for targeted youth. She announces that the Guild will seek a Leadership Initiative grant from NEA to support partnerships between community schools and public housing partners. The Guild would provide training, mentoring, and technical assistance. Gloria explains about the Resident Opportunities and Self Sufficiency Grant (ROSS) program of supportive services. She also points out that the monies must be obligated by the end of the federal fiscal year on 9/30/2000.

May 25, 2000 – A follow-up conference call is held with Scott, Michael McLaughlin (Director, Millennium Projects and Leadership Initiatives, NEA); Lee Kessler (Director of Federal Partnerships, NEA), Lolita, and Jonathan. Lolita explains that HUD wants a partnership with another federal agency. They need to know how serious NEA is about this initiative. Lolita passes on HUD's requirement about obligating the funds before September 30th.

May 30, 2000 – A conference call takes place with Gloria, Paula Blunt (Associate Deputy Secretary in charge of the ROSS program), Lolita, and Jonathan to discuss the possible outline of a partnership: HUD will transfer funds to NEA, which will contract with the Guild to carry out the project, following their standard grants process. Gloria and Paula say it sounds good to them.

June 8, 2000 – The Guild submits a project outline to Gloria and follows up with a conference call with Scott, Lee, Gloria, Paula, Lolita, and Jonathan. The purpose of the call is to explore the basics of a cooperative agreement with NEA, HUD, and the Guild. The group notes that everyone is on the same page. Moreover, HUD has checked with their general counsel who approves. HUD's Assistant Secretary is also interested.

June 21, 2000 – Lolita calls Scott to talk about the modalities regarding the involvement of State Arts Agencies based on continuing consultations with Jonathan Katz. Scott points out that "we must get it together quickly."

June 24, 2000 – New Advisory Group[5] meets with Grady Hillman, Joanne Williams, Wendy Fleisher, Lolita, and Jonathan.

July 20, 2000 12:19 pm – Lolita to Lee Kessler

Subject Creative Communities

I also want to share with you some good news – we received the first response yesterday to our requests for matching funds. The Mellon Foundation emailed us to let us know that they have approved $50,000 toward the match. I thought you'd like to know.

July 20, 2000 5:31 pm – Lee to Lolita

Subject: Creative Communities

Congratulations! I know that everyone here will be so pleased to hear about the Mellon Foundation. Everything went great this morning. Council members liked the project and expressed their support. The actual proposal will be voted on tomorrow. I will keep you posted.

July 24, 2000 1:42 pm – Lee to Lolita

Subject: Creative Communities Council Meeting

Congratulations! Clear sailing with the Council. Let's hope the wind continues to stay at our backs and we just glide forward to a successful program. Again, congratulations. I hope everyone at the Guild is celebrating.

July 24, 2000 4:19 pm – Lolita to Lee

Subject: Creative Communities

Wonderful news about the Council and real cause for celebration! The Irish have a saying: may the sun be on your back and the road rise up to meet you. So here's to clear sailing, wind, sun, road, mixed metaphors and all…! Thanks a million for everything, Lee.

September 5, 2000 – Jonathan Katz sends a letter to Gloria thanking her for meeting with the Board of Directors of the National Assembly of State Arts Agencies (NASAA). He writes, "Your participation really helped us to understand the value of state arts agency participation with HUD, the National Guild of Community Schools of the Arts, and the NEA in the Leadership Initiative…. As you know the NASAA Board of Directors adopted a resolution to support the developing partnership…as manifested in the Arts Access/National Leadership Initiative. Furthermore, the NASAA board and staff resolved to serve as a liaison between the Initiative and the state arts agencies."

September 11, 2000 – Paula Blunt and Beverly Hardy call to inform us that HUD is shooting for the end of the fiscal year. They emphasize that the program is a priority and on the "top of their plate." They advise us that the review of pieces has just started and apologize for the delay. They emphasize that the money will not be lost. Nevertheless, we start to worry.

September 13, 2000 – Lolita calls Tony Tighe (Coordinator, Federal Partnerships, National Endowment for the Arts) who says that: As of noon today, [he's had] no response from HUD. [He] must have sign-off regarding cooperative agreement. Scott called HUD [and was] told that Gloria is out of town, due to a bereavement in the family. Scott informed Beverly that HUD must get back to her by the end of the day.

September 15, 2000 3:40 pm – Beverly Hardy to Tony Tighe, forwarded to all parties at NEA and NGCSA 4:48 pm.

I will attempt to reach you from Kansas City. I am taking your materials with me. You can expect a call from me by Tuesday [September 19].

September 15, 2000 4:39 pm – Tony Tighe to all parties at NEA

Jonathan just called and reported that Beverly Hardy of HUD will be on [sic] travel Monday through Wednesday of next week. Beverly said HUD still wanted to transfer the funds this year and that she would try to use her "airplane time" to review the draft....Don't know what else we can do than keep knocking.

September 25, 2000 12:11 pm – Jonathan to Jeraldine White

Subject: Creative Communities Documents

I've asked Michael McLaughlin, the leader of the project team at NEA, to send you via email the most current versions of the three primary documents we are working on....The documents are: Interagency Agreement between HUD and NEA; Cooperative Agreement between NEA and the Guild; NEA's Guidelines for Applicants....Lolita and I are available all day to discuss any questions you might have.

September 25, 2000, 12:53 pm –Tony Tighe to Jeraldine White

Cc: to all parties at NEA, HUD, and National Guild

Subject: NEA-HUD-NGCSA documents

URGENT. At your request, attached are the following documents all of which were prepared on the assumption that HUD would transfer $3 million to the Endowment: $2.7 million in direct grants and $300,000 to the National Guild of Community Schools of the Arts to coordinate technical assistance for the grantees.

September 27, 2000 – With time running short, Lolita convenes a meeting at HUD for senior management from NEA, HUD, and the Guild in order to review the paperwork in person and sign documents.

It is three days before the end of the federal fiscal year. In some instances, documents need to be typed or retyped. Present are: Scott Shanklin-Peterson, Lee Kessler, Michael McLaughlin, Beverly Hardy, Paula Blunt (who signs on behalf of Gloria Cousar), Jeraldine White, Jonathan, and Lolita. The group waits patiently at the table for several hours until all the relevant documents are produced and signed by all present. The countdown to September 30 begins and nerves begin to fray. Just a day's holdup could mean the collapse of the entire project.

September 29, 2000 – Lolita places a call to Ron Simon, NEA budget officer. Ron says there is no way the money can get transferred in time to get the cooperative agreement. He assumes HUD will make obligation on their end in 2000 and pick up in 2001. Lolita is told that Beverly faxed the interagency agreement at 4:30 pm on September 28.

September 29, 2000 – Paula Blunt calls the Guild to report that everything has been signed and an e-mail has been sent to all parties at HUD to complete the process. [HUD] is going forward to obligate funds – for all funds, not just NGCSA. Lolita is told that HUD staff will be at work on Saturday, September 30, the last day of the fiscal year. Now everyone just has to trust that all the formalities will be completed within the next 24 hours. There is nothing more any of us can do but wait while on tenterhooks.

October 4, 2000 4:20 pm – Michael McLaughlin to Beverly Hardy

Subject: Creative Communities paperwork

Scott asked me to let you know that the Creative Communities guidelines must be sent to the printer on Friday morning (10/6/00). If edits are not received by close of business on Thursday, we'll assume everything is fine....As you know, we've all agreed that on-site instructional activity will begin with the 2001 school year. I'm afraid an ever-tightening timeline during which we must assist applicants, conduct a rigorous selection process, and coordinate in-depth technical assistance.

October 6, 2000 5:13 pm – Tony Tighe to all parties at NEA and NGCSA

Subject: HUD lives!

Lolita called me and reported that she had spoken to Beverly and that Beverly said that Paula Blunt's signature for Gloria Cousar was sufficient to obligate the funds for HUD.... I would suggest that it's time to ask Finance to attempt to draw down the funds. If the transfer doesn't work, we'll know we have a problem; if it works, we're all set for now.

October 6, 2000 5:26 pm – Tony Tighe to all parties at NEA and NGCSA

No subject given

Just after my 5:08 message to y'all, I received an email from Beverly Hardy with her edit to the Creative Communities guidelines as an attachment. So here is my reply to Beverly (an attempt to summarize where we are now) with her message and the revision as an attachment. Now I won't have to walk the halls delivering hard copy.

Enjoy!

October 17, 2000 1:44 pm – Lolita Mayadas to Michael McLaughlin

Subject: Memo to field et al

We are sending out a mailing to the field on Thursday and I would like to include a brief notification of the Creative Communities project in advance so people can begin to plan.

I also spoke with Bill Hummel [at NEA] today about the Cooperative Agreement. He said he is waiting for confirmation from your Budget Office that the monies have been transferred and gave me to understand that there were no hitches. He also agreed to send me the executed agreement by overnight mail as soon as Scott has signed it.

October 17, 2000 3:42 pm – Tony Tighe to all parties at NEA and NGCSA

Subject: ACTUALLY GETTING HUD's MONEY!!!!

An interagency agreement worksheet is making the rounds through offices today and should arrive in Budget and Finance by tomorrow with the accompanying interagency agreement. Hopefully, the lady in Texas will have all the answers we need.

October 20, 2000 3:21 pm – Beverly Hardy to Tony Tighe

Subject: Finance Information

Hello, you should be able to draw down the $3 million today or tomorrow. I notified Teena Neptune that this would happen soon. Teena is my contact in Finance and Accounting (Fort Worth, TX) on this.

October 20, 2000 3:28 pm – Tony Tighe to all parties at NEA and NGCSA

Subject: HUD Money

Lois [from NEA] has drawn down the $3 million from HUD. As she explained it to me, we now wait to see if anyone at HUD notices and complains. That can be within a week or at the end of the month. But Beverly assured us that the funds were obligated, so there should be no problems, eh?

October 25, 2000 4:22 pm – Paul Carlson (NEA Finance Office) to Tony Tighe

Subject: HUD money

We have received the $3 million from HUD for Creative Communities and posted it to the appropriate account.

October 25, 2000 5:03 pm –Tony Tighe to all parties NGCSA and NEA

Yayyy!!!

October 27, 2000 12:32 pm – Scott Shanklin-Peterson to all parties NEA and NGCSA

Subject: HUD money

CONGRATULATIONS!

Thanks to the energy and enthusiasm of every member of the team, the process was complete and the program could move forward as planned. The Guild recognizes with great appreciation the following individuals who played key roles in designing, developing, and implementing the Initiative:

HUD	NEA	National Guild	Advisory Group
Gloria Cousar	Scott Shanklin-Peterson	Lolita Mayadas	Wendy Fleischer
Paula Blunt	Lee Kessler	Jonathan Herman	Grady Hillman
Beverly Hardy	Michael McLaughlin	Shawn Dove	Joanne Williams
Jeraldine White		Susanne Sousa	Camille Akeju
			Latetia Ramirez

The next step was to open the competitive grants process to applications from all 50 states with the proviso that 20 sites from 20 US cities would be selected by a special panel appointed by the NEA. By the time of the deadline, 115 applications from 39 states had been received. And subsequently, a three-day panel meeting to select the sites took place at NEA's offices from January 29-31, 2001. Lolita Mayadas, Jonathan Herman, and Shawn Dove from the National Guild were also invited to audit the process and to provide material information where needed. Each application was meticulously reviewed by the panel through several rounds with final choices determined by the quality of the applications, geographic diversity, and other NEA criteria. At the end of the process, 20 schools in 20 different states were awarded $135,000 which required a 25% match. The total amount of direct grants to be disbursed was $2,700,000. Each selected site was eligible for participation in the full program of training and technical assistance.[6] Subsequently, the first Training Institute, entitled *Building Bridges, Building the Brand, Building the Bucks*, was held from July 12-15, 2001. We were pleased that the Institute received highly positive reviews from both participants and observers and provided valuable feedback.

Five years later, in 2006, a detailed and thorough evaluation of the program was carried out by Bruce Jones. Excerpts from the Introduction and Conclusion of the Summary Report follow:

Introduction

Creative Communities is a ground-breaking initiative to bring high-quality arts instruction to underserved children and youth in public housing communities. Developed in 2001 as a collaboration among the National Guild for Community Schools of the Arts, the US Department of Housing and Urban Development (HUD), and the National Endowment for the Arts (NEA), the Initiative (CCI) was the first-ever collaboration between NEA and HUD and represented a $4.65 million investment in, and commitment to, community arts education.

Conclusion of the Evaluation Report

The Creative Communities Initiative (CCI) demonstrated that a unique concept, implemented with skill, patience, and goodwill, can be turned into a transformative experience for children and families living in public housing communities. The Initiative showed that bringing rigorous, high-quality arts programming to underserved children and youth is a viable way to nurture and promote their artistic and human development, their inner spirit as human beings, and, in the long run, the well-being of their communities.[7]

The larger lesson of CCI, though, is that making this kind of programming an enduring component of the services offered to children in public housing is a challenge that requires careful planning and a strong, flexible partnership. Findings from the CCI evaluation, condensed and summarized in this report, provide a roadmap of sorts for community schools of the arts to follow as they pursue partnerships with public housing authorities, as well as with other public or private entities. Thankfully, this is a path that others have traveled as well, and they have shared their wisdom through a variety of documents, many of which can easily be obtained online from the National Guild.

Chapter Eighteen
Transitions

Now this is not the end. It is not even the beginning of the end. But it is, perhaps, the end of the beginning.

– Winston Churchill

My many years of service as Executive Director of the Guild had given me an insider's view of the growth patterns of dozens of emerging and mid-size arts education institutions. This chapter attempts to spell out how those experiences relate to the Guild and to my decision to retire.

I have come to believe that the life cycles of leaders are inevitably linked to the life cycles of organizations and vice-versa. The fact is that few individuals possess all of the skills and attributes it takes to be an effective leader through every stage of organizational growth. At the early "start-up" stage, an institution needs, and typically attracts, a leader who is generally a risk-taker and visionary. But as the organization changes and grows, this top-down style of entrepreneurial management becomes less and less productive. The Guild had counseled so many institutions that were going through transitions. We knew what it entailed. So it didn't need much reflection for me to realize that succession to new leadership had now become necessary for the Guild.

To my mind, the Guild had simply grown beyond my capacity to manage it. This was not a noble or self-sacrificing posture but simply a pragmatic recognition of my own interests, capabilities, and limitations. In reality, I was not excited by the prospect of being an administrator charged with fashioning and maintaining a corporate-style organization. To achieve that goal, I believed the Guild needed a person schooled in management skills and team building, someone with the ability to delegate responsibility (not just tasks) and a knack for creating consensus. That new job description was not for me. Besides, the take-charge style I had adopted in the early years seemed out of sync with the "new" Guild.

Anyhow, I missed the "old" Guild. I missed the freedom of driving solo, the sense of community, and the satisfaction of bringing people to the table – the missionary zeal, if you will. Given the Guild's near-death condition when I was hired in 1981, I had no option but to function like a sort of founder-director. But now, having helped to bring it to this place, I was neither qualified nor motivated by the prospect of leading what the Guild was becoming. It had been a joyous, challenging, and deeply rewarding journey, but I couldn't change, or perhaps I simply didn't want to.

Having considered all the pros and cons, I informed the Board at the end of the year 2000 about my intention to retire on December 31, 2001. Azim also decided to retire at the same time. With that, a Search Committee[1] was formed under the leadership of Lowell Noteboom, and Cathy French, who headed the Catherine French Group, was hired as the Search Consultant. Cathy placed ads primarily in the college circuit communication channels, and she received responses from several administrators in the network. Few of them, if any, had worked at a community school of the arts. The Search Committee worked long and hard and interviewed several candidates. At the end of that process, they presented their preferred candidate, Bill Fellenberg, to the Board, which confirmed his appointment. Bill was Senior Deputy Director and Chief Financial Officer at <u>Montclair Art Museum</u> in New Jersey. The committee felt that his "background and experience, while not in a community school setting [gave] him a skill set and perspective that would serve the National Guild well."[2]

Concurrently with this decision, the Board also began to explore the possibility of moving back to New York where the Guild was incorporated. There were several reasons why this made sense. First, the Guild had only moved from New York to the Mayadas home in New Jersey for reasons of expediency in 1981. As a result, it was no longer eligible to receive grants from the New York State Council for the Arts. And since the Guild was not incorporated in New Jersey, it could not get grants from the New Jersey State Arts Council either. In a nutshell, since we were incorporated in one state and resident in another, we were not eligible for funding from either arts agency. Therefore, the decision in 2002 to establish a "home" in New York again made eminent sense.

So with great enthusiasm and energy, Guild staff began to look for new space in New York City. It was an exciting opportunity but it certainly carried its own challenges. After looking at several different sites, the staff eventually settled on a building under construction at 520 8th Avenue – a few blocks from Penn Station – where a large space on the third floor was available. Dividers for cubicles would have to be constructed, but after detailed negotiations a contract was signed, and the Guild moved into brand new premises in 2002.

Meanwhile, I had been thinking about the future of the Creative Communities Initiative. Many of us in the Guild and elsewhere felt it was too important an initiative to be allowed to fade out after its first iteration. I was also concerned that lessons learned would be lost even though they had been documented. Moreover, I was not confident that the program would continue under the new Executive Director. Given these factors, I offered to stay on as Consultant for Creative Communities for a year or two. I thought this would give grant makers and the NEA some confidence that the program would keep going under known and experienced leadership. When I made an informal proposal to Bill Fellenberg, he was in favor of it. However, after some thought I dropped the idea since I was uncertain as to what kind of support structure would be available to me, especially on the staffing and development side.

The transition to new leadership was led by Katherine Schumacher, Chairman of the Guild's Board beginning in 1998. Her term as Chair would extend through Bill Fellenberg's first year as Executive Director. Kathy's background was exactly suited to lead us through this major change. She was active in her community in the service of the arts, education, and healthcare fields, and had served on several Boards, including the Rochester Philharmonic Orchestra, The Genesee Hospital, and the Hochstein School of Music, which she had chaired in the early 1990's. In her professional life, she taught English courses at the Rochester Institute of Technology and was Writing Director in its College of Liberal Arts. Kathy also pursued her interest in music as a student in the Voice Department at Hochstein and was a member of several choral groups.

In paying tribute to her, I can do no better than to quote from my citation at the time Kathy received the President's Award [3] in Pittsburgh in 2005:

Many are the times I have sat at the head table at these conferences in the Executive Director's chair, now so ably occupied by Jonathan Herman. And many are the Presidents and Chairmen I have worked with from Henry Bridges in 1981 through to Kathy Schumacher in 2001, the year Azim and I retired. The Guild has been singularly lucky to have had people of great dedication and commitment serving in these leadership positions. Each has brought to the Guild his or her own particular style and vision. Each has seen us through periods of great change and growth. Each has brought fresh thinking to the Guild and access to new networks. All have left their stamp on the organization.

But for Kathy I have a special affection and admiration. We were luckier to get [her] than we realized in those days. When she first became a trustee, we knew we were getting a lady in the true sense of the word, with all the qualities of grace and civility that word implies. But what we didn't know about then was her courage, her determination, and inner strength – qualities she amply displayed as we got to know her a little better.

More importantly, Kathy knew what it meant to be a board chairman. She knew her job, she knew the board's job, and she knew mine. She never, ever interfered with staff responsibilities. For that alone, she should get a medal...! Her expectations were clear and professional, and she never shirked a job that needed to be done. She was as generous of spirit as she was with her time and personal resources. And she was as steady as a rock. Through good times and bad, she had a calming influence on all of us. It was a joy to work with her.

One of the highlights of 2001, in personal terms, was the President's Award given jointly to Azim and me for "visionary leadership and exceptional service to the National Guild and the community arts education movement." The nomination for the award was made by Steve Shapiro, Executive Director of San Francisco's Community Music Center. Speaking for myself at the New York conference, I tried to express my great appreciation for this singular honor:

You cannot imagine how much this award means to me because it's a tribute from my peers, people I have worked with for decades. And for me that is more meaningful than any other award could possibly be. I will treasure this for what it signifies, and as a reminder of a period that was, and is, one of the most satisfying and enriching of my life.

As Robert Frost once said, "Yield who will to their separation – my object is to unite my avocation and my vocation as my two eyes make one in sight." And some benevolent and unknown destiny has allowed that to happen for me.

My only regret is that I haven't finished in 20 years what I really wanted to get finished. But I do plan to get it all done in the six weeks I have left. Procrastination is no longer an option!

Over this whole weekend I've been incredibly honored and valued and fussed over. As you can imagine, there's nothing quite so wonderful as people telling you how wonderful you are.

[But as] Yo Yo Ma once said, when asked about all his rave reviews, "When you believe your own press you're really in trouble."

Nevertheless, this is my chance, my last chance, to thank you for your generous praise and for giving me so much credit for achievements, which are really a reflection of the work we have all done together.

So thank you for all your support, your comradeship, your gifts, your letters, and expressions of support.

I will treasure them all.

There was nothing that would ever top that experience. I spent the next several weeks in a nostalgic mood, tying up loose ends and closing out unfinished jobs. Then, on December 31, my last day, I remember going back to the office one more time. I collected a few personal things and looked around the work place which had been such a large part of my life for so long. It had been an exhilarating journey, filled with all manner of achievements and challenges, and so many good memories. But now it was over. I opened the front door, switched off the light, and closed the door behind me. This was the end of an era for me...and the start of a new one for the Guild.

PHOTOS[*]

---

[*] All of the photos in this section are courtesy of the National Guild.

Lolita Mayadas

1983

L-R: Allen Sapp, Frank Hodsoll, Chairman, National Endowment for the Arts.

1984

L-R: Monroe Levin presents the Guild's Leadership Award to Lester Glick.

1985

Olympia Halle, Munich, Germany. European Youth Festival.

1985

Herbert Zipper, Los Angeles, CA.

1987

**First National Festival of the Arts, Carnegie Hall. Youth Jazz
Band with Wynton Marsalis, solo trumpet.**

1991

L-R: Jessica Chao, Program Director, Wallace Funds; Jane Ballard. New York, NY. (Photo: Martha Swope.)

1991

L-R: Jessica Chao, Lolita Mayadas, Carl Atkins celebrating Lolita Mayadas' 10th anniversary with the Guild.

1991

**L-R: Herbert Zipper, Lolita Mayadas, Jane Ballard, Carl Shaver.
St. Louis, MO.**

1992

Board members, L-R: Seated on the arm of the sofa: Eileen Cline. Standing: Virginia Lawrence, Carl Atkins, David Lapin, Henry Bridges, Barbara Field, Sheila McKenna, Robert Capanna, Laura Calzolari, Ron Banyay, John Sutherland, Charles Farmer. Seated on radiator: Eric Bachrach. Seated on the sofa, L-R: Iona Benson, Janet Hunt, Toby Mayman, Fran Zarubick, Jacob Landau. Seated on the floor:Carol Dickert and Staff members, Lolita Mayadas, Azim Mayadas. San Francisco, CA.

1994

Ilene Mack, Senior Program Officer, Hearst Foundation, hands a check over to Lolita Mayadas for the Guild's Endowment Fund. New York, NY.

1994

Second National Festival of the Arts. National Guild Youth Orchestra. Conductor: Lukas Foss. John F. Kennedy Center for the Performing Arts, Washington, DC. (Photo: Claire Flanders.)

1994

Henry Bridges. (Photo: Claire Flanders.)

1994

Lolita and Azim Mayadas. (Photo: Claire Flanders.)

1994

**L-R: Robert Capanna, Laure Calzolari, Elmar Oliveira.
(Photo: Claire Flanders.)**

1994

Carl Atkins presents the Leadership Award to Scott Shanklin Peterson who accepts it on behalf of Jane Alexander, Chairman, National Endowment for the Arts, Washington, DC. (Photo: Claire Flanders.)

1994

**Student Performers — green room of the John F. Kennedy Center
for the Performing Arts, Washington, DC.
(Photo: Claire Flanders.)**

1995

**Jonathan Herman (center) with Arts Management in Community
Institutions (AMICI) class.**

1995

Guild Staff, Englewood, NJ. L-R: Jonathan Herman, Lolita Mayadas, Azim Mayadas, Alison Rubin, Kate Brackett, Claudio Knafo, Angela Dayrit.

1998

**L-R: Van Cliburn, Gayle Morgan, Angel Ramon Rivera —
recipient of the Guild's Service Award. Dallas, TX.**

2001

L-R: Iona Benson, Lydia Kontos. New York, NY.

2001

Kathy Schumacher. New York, NY.

Undated

Howard Klein.

Undated

Richard Evans.

Lolita Mayadas

Notes

Foreword

1   Lowell Noteboom, National Guild Trustee 1996-2016; Chair, Arts for All Strategic Planning Committee, National Guild, 1999-2003. Partner and Associate General Counsel, Stinson LLP, Minneapolis; Leadership roles on boards of several leading music organizations.

2   Excerpted from remarks made by Lowell Noteboom in 2016 upon his accepting the National Guild's Service Award which recognizes "exceptional service to the National Guild and the community arts education movement." https://www.youtube.com/watch?v=Hlm4wA11KYU&t=28s

Preface

1   Robert Egan – Music and the Arts in the Community: The Community Music School in America Page xi

Chapter One: Prologue

1.   Robert Egan – Music and the Arts in the Community: The Community Music School in America Page xi

2.   Ibid. 151

3.   Charter Members, as noted in *A Retrospective* [dated November 1995] by Azim L. Mayadas; *Note: many of the charter schools have subsequently changed their names*:

    a.   All Newton Music School, West Newton, MA; Boston Music School Settlement, MA; Brooklyn Music School Settlement, NY; The Cleveland Music School Settlement, OH; Community Music Schools Foundation, St Louis, MO; First Settlement Music School, Buffalo, NY; Manhattan

School of Music, New York, NY; Music School Settlement, New York, NY; The Settlement Music School, Philadelphia, PA; South End Music School, Boston, MA; Turtle Bay Music School, New York, NY; Wilmington Music School, Wilmington, DE.

4. Robert Egan – Music and the Arts in the Community: The Community Music School in America. 248.

5. Ibid., 249-250.

6. Ibid., 251.

7. Ibid., 257.

8. Board Minutes June 15, 1967.

9. Peggy Quackenbush email July 11, 2001.

10. Board Minutes May 3, 1971.

Chapter Two: Grand Design

1. *Classic Feynman – All the Adventures of a Curious Character.* Richard P. Feynman.

2. Robert Egan – Music and the Arts in the Community: The Community Music School in America. 254.

3. Kal Novak Interview September 18, 2003.

4. Robert Egan – Music and the Arts in the Community: The Community Music School in America. 275.

5. Paul Cummins – Dachau Song: The Twentieth Century Odyssey of Herbert Zipper. 85.

6. Wikipedia – 7/12/2020. en.wikipedia.org/wiki/Jura Soyfer.

7. Richard W. Colburn email dated October 22, 2020.

8. Toby Mayman as quoted in the Los Angeles Times obituary by Claudia Luther, June 4, 2004.

9. Richard W. Colburn email dated October 22, 2020.

10. Los Angeles Times obituary by Claudia Luther, June 4, 2004.

11. Robert Egan – Music and the Arts in the Community: The Community Music School in America. 287.

12. Kal Novak Interview September 18, 2003.

13. Robert Egan – Music and the Arts in the Community: The Community Music School in America. 271.

14. Ibid., 292.

15. Ibid., 288.

16. Board Minutes May 21, 1973.

17. Arts for All Fund. Board Meeting March 10, 1971. The initial goals of the Fund were to expand the membership to new schools, strengthen member schools and raise a national endowment for the benefit of the schools and the national office.

18. Board Minutes May 3, 1971

19. Robert Egan – Music and the Arts in the Community: The Community Music School in America. 268.

20. Kal Novak Interview September 11, 2003.

21. Executive Director Report May 11, 1972.

22. Zipper Letter to Membership May 16, 1972

23. Board Minutes January 25, 1972.

24. Ibid.

25. Ibid.

26. Ibid.

27. Ibid.

28. Board Minutes May 1, 1972: Publication of Teaching Materials based on Afro-American Piano Music [Annual Meeting – 1970] a proposal for an institute for the study of "rock" in cooperation with MENC [Annual Meeting – 1970] a plan for an Objective Study of a Music-oriented Primary Education [Annual Meeting May 1, 1972] and a $100,000 project to

provide training and career education for minority students [Annual Conference, St. Louis, MI, November 1971 – Reports and Minutes].

29. Kal Novak Interview September 11, 2003.

30. Annual Meeting Minutes, May 1, 1972.

31. Membership Listing 1972.

32. Richard Casper – "keen sense of loss." Letter to Lolita and Azim Mayadas 2001.

33. Harris Danziger – Letter to the Membership, January 31, 1972.

Chapter Three: A New Era Begins

1. The Hollow Men, T.S. Eliot.

2. Arts Reporting Service January 10, 1972.

3. Robert Egan – Music and the Arts in the Community: The Community Music School in America. 297.

4. Chuck Mark Letter early September 1972 (undated).

5. Robert Egan – Music and the Arts in the Community: The Community Music School in America. 298.

6. Carl Shaver Report, May 1, 1972.

7. Robert Egan – Music and the Arts in the Community: The Community Music School in America. 301

8. Carl Shaver: *Funding Guidelines*.

9. Halsey North Interview August 21, 2006.

10. Annual Meeting Minutes October 11, 1972.

11. Nominations for the expanded board were: Arnold Gingrich, Chairman and Publisher, Esquire, Inc., New York, NY, Edward Bernays, President, Bernays Foundation, Boston, MA, Abe Fortas, Partner, Fortas & Koven, Attorneys, Washington, D.C., John H. MacFadyen, President, Associated Councils of the Arts, New York, NY, David Melnikoff, Vice President, The Federal Reserve Bank of

Philadelphia, PA, Dr. Merle Montgomery, Vice President, Carl Fischer, Inc. New York, NY, Colonel Samuel R. Rosenbaum, Trustee, Music Performance Trust Funds (1948-70), Philadelphia, PA, Roger Stevens, Chairman of the Board, John F. Kennedy Center for the Performing Arts, Washington, D.C., and Paul Fromm, the philanthropist.

12. Board Minutes January 25, 1972.

13. Charles Mark, undated. Prepared for 1972 conference.

14. Music Performance Trust Funds (MPTF). Colonel Samuel Rosenbaum, an MPTF trustee, arranged for payments by MPTF to be made to students at National Guild schools for performances. Students were encouraged to donate the checks to the National Guild. Rosenbaum, a leading Philadelphia attorney, was a trustee of the Philadelphia Orchestra during the Stokowski and Ormandy years. He established the Music Performance Trust Fund to subsidize live music performances.

15. Board Minutes August 21, 1973.

16. A school must offer professionally directed organized instruction in one or more art forms in a manner which allows the student to progress from his (sic) initial entry level toward the mastery of the art form; it must provide a faculty of teachers recognized within their profession by their peers; it must insure that students have the proper equipment and materials for instruction, and facilities adequate for the learning process; it must serve, within reason, all persons in the community eager to study at the school without regard for the ability to pay for instruction; it must also welcome, encourage, and make possible enrollment of persons of all ethnic, racial and social groups in its near and greater community.

17. In November 1972 a Task Force consisting of Carl Shaver, Charles Mark, Kal Novak, Susan Hill, Bernie Jackson, Sam Herr and Dorothy Maynor was formed and charged with developing a set of requirements for Guild membership. An

excerpt from their criteria for full membership is given in Item 16 above.

18. Board Minutes 2/9/1973.

19. Board Minutes 5/31/1973 – Kal Novak Report.

20. Robert Egan – Music and the Arts in the Community: The Community Music School in America. 301.

21. Kal Novak Interview 9/2003.

22. Board Minutes 5/21/1973.

23. Board Minutes 11/12/1973

24. Carl Shaver Memo 3/12/1974.

25. Board Minutes 11/12/1973.

26. Halsey North Interview 8/21/2006.

27. Robert Egan – Music and the Arts in the Community: The Community Music School in America. 321.

28. Halsey North Interview 8/21/2006.

Chapter Four: A Parting of the Ways

1 Lawrence Peter "Yogi" Berra (May 12, 1925 – September 22, 2015) was an American professional baseball catcher, who later took on the roles manager and coach.

2 Board Minutes 9/11/1973.

3 Board Minutes 11/12/1973.

4 Dorothy Amarandos letter dated 1/21/1974.

5 Exec. Committee minutes 1/21/1974.

6 A general booklet on the scope and intent of the movement that could be used to cultivate individuals, corporations and other funding sources. Narrative Supplement to NEA Grant. Request 01/18/1974.

7 Robert Egan – Music and the Arts in the Community: The Community Music School in America. 306.

8   Board Minutes 11/12/1973.

9   Dorothy Amarandos Interview 9/5/2006.

10 Board meeting November 1973.

11 Dorothy Amarandos Interview 09/5/2006.

12 Fundraising Plan for the National Guild 3/12/1974.

13 Carl Shaver Letter to Dorothy Amarandos 3/18/1974.

14 Ibid.,

15 Dorothy Amarandos Rebuttal letter 3/28/1974.

16 Carl Shaver letter to to Dorothy Maynor. 3/26/1974.

17 Executive Committee Minutes 3/28/1974.

18 Dorothy Amarandos – letter to Board 8/12/1974.

19 Dorothy Amarandos Interview 9/5/2006.

20 Dorothy Amarandos Letter to Guild Board 5/31/1974.

21 Dorothy Amarandos Interview 9/5/2006.

22 Board Minutes 5/7/1974.

23 Robert Egan – Music and the Arts in the Community: The
    Community Music School in America. 310.

24 Partial transcript of Advisors' Meeting 10/20/1975.

25 Minutes of Joint Meeting September 1974.

26 Annual Meeting Minutes November 1978.

27 Board Minutes 11/12/1974.

28 Ibid.

29 Dorothy Amarandos Letter to the Board 1/30/1975.

30 Hartford meeting 7-23 through 7-25, 1975

31 Dorothy Amarandos Interview 2006.

32 Richard Casper Interview12/19/2003.

33 Dorothy Amarandos Interview 9/5/2006.

Chapter Five: Turning Point

1. Heraclitus of Ephesus was a pre-Socratic Greek philosopher, and a native of the city of Ephesus. Heraclitus was famous for his insistence on ever-present change as being the fundamental essence of the universe, as stated in the famous saying, "No man ever steps in the same river twice" (see "panta rhei", "everything flows"). [Wikipedia 8/13/2017].

2. Marcy Horwitz Interview 9/23/2005.

3. Ibid.

4. Dorothy Amarandos Interview 10/16/2006.

5. Executive Committee Meeting 6/1/1977.

6. Richard Casper Interview 12/10/2003.

7. Annual Meeting minutes 11/29/1977.

8. Marcy Horwitz Interview 9/23/2005.

9. Board Minutes 1/18/1980.

10. Ibid.

11. Music Teachers National Association, National Association of Schools of Music, Very Special Arts, Young Audiences, Young Audiences, Arts-in-Hospitals, College Music Society. [Marcy Horwitz email 9-26-2005].

12. Roundtable of the Arts, Kennedy Center's National Black Music Colloquium and Competition, the Gifted and Talented Task Force, and the NEA's Task Force on the training and development of young performing artists. The Guild was also recognized in the seminal "Coming to Our Senses," Report issued by a panel of eminent citizens and chaired by David Rockefeller Jr. [Marcy Horwitz email 9-26-2005].

13. Ernest Dyson – Report from Washington, November 1978.

14. Annual Meeting Minutes 11/1978.

15. Lester Glick Report – Annual Meeting, 11/1978.

16. Ibid.

17. Marcy Horwitz Interview 9/25/2005.

18. Lester Glick Report – Annual Meeting, 11/1978.

19. Executive Committee Minutes 9/11/1979.

20. Marcy Horwitz Interview 10/10/2005.

21. Financial Statement : Sandra Kaplan, 4/9/1980.

22. Marcy Horwitz Memo to Finance Committee 7/22/1980.

23. Marcy Horwitz email to Lolita Mayadas 9/26/2006.

Chapter Six: The New Hire

1. William Shakespeare Henry V, Act III, Scene I.

2. Robert Christiansen letter to Board 6/21/1981.

3. Executive Committee Minutes 7/6/1981.

4. Henry Bridges letter to Allen Sapp 7/16/1981.

5. Henry Bridges Interview 10/21/2005.

6. Henry Bridges Appointment letter 7/15/1981.

7. Henry Bridges Interview 10/21/2005.

8. Hadassah Markson Interview 11/02/2005.

9. Undated comment by Annetta Kaplan to Lolita Mayadas.

10. The proposals included:

- Formation of a National Advisory Council.

- Instituting an Annual Membership Drive.

- Establishing a Fundraising Committee and a P.R. Committee.

- Expanding and amplifying programs and services to the field. (Specifics were included).

- Appointing Regional Reps and a volunteer corps to help out in the office.

- Reappointing a Guild representative to communicate with federal decision makers and arts, labor, and educational constituencies.

- Improving the quality and quantity of publications, statistical reports, and manuals.

- Every Board member appointed to a standing committee by Board Chair, Henry Bridges.

- Every committee charged with establishing goals and objectives and strategies to achieve them.

Chapter Seven: The Path Forward

1. "The question is not when we came here...but why our families came here. And what we did after we arrived." Jimmy (James Earl Carter, former President of the United States), speech at Al Smith Dinner. October 26, 1976. Bartlett's Quotations 1992.

2. Allen Sapp letter to Lolita Mayadas 10/28/1981.

3. Board Minutes 10/15/1981.

4. Susan's husband, Raymond, was on the Board of the Guild.

5. Lolita Mayadas memo to Richard Letts 6/1/1982.

Chapter Eight: Candles in the Dark

1. Kalman Novak, Director of the Music Institute of Chicago, Winnetka, Illinois. Board member and one-time Treasurer of the National Guild. Phone Interview: 9/11/2003.

2. Henry Bridges Report Annual Meeting 11/16/1982

3. Wikipedia 12/31/2017

4. Charles Ulrick and Josephine Bay Foundation, now the Bay and Paul Foundations.

5. Steering Committee: **David. E. Myers**, (Committee Chair), Director of the Center for Education Partnerships in Music, Associate Director of the School of Music, Georgia State

University, Atlanta; **Ronne Hartfield**, Consultant and former Executive Director of Museum Education, Art Institute of Chicago and Urban Gateways; **Jane Remer**, Author and Consultant, **Larry Scripp**, Director, Music-in-Education Program and Research Center for Learning Through Music, New England Conservatory of Music; **Andrea Temkin**, Executive Director, Community School of Music and Arts, Mountain View, California.

6. Board Meeting Minutes 2/4/1983.

Chapter Nine: *Quo Vadis*

1. *Quo Vadis* – Latin for "Whither goest thou?" The Polish writer Henryk Sienkiewicz authored the novel *Narrative of the Time of Nero* (1895) which in turn has been made into motion pictures several times, including a 1951 version that was nominated for eight Academy Awards.

2. President George W. Bush on the occasion of Katrina Hurricane Recovery efforts. New Orleans, Sept. 2005.

3. Monroe Levin Letter dated 1/3/1984.

4. Board Minutes 2/19/84.

5. Ibid.

6. Lewis Carroll – Brainy Quote 6/8/2018

7. Fund Drive dated 6/6/1984.

8. Helen Jackson memo to institutional members dated 1/23/1984.

9. Robert Capanna memo to institutional members

10. Board Minutes 2/4/1984.

11. Fundraising Committee Report 10/30/1984.

12. NEA Staff members present: Renee Levine, Inter-Arts Program; Joan Armstrong, Program Specialist, Inter-Arts Program; Paul Fran, Assistant Director, Music Program.

13. Monroe Levin memo to the Board 2/17/1984.

Chapter Ten: New Horizons

1. Margaret Spellings, former United States Secretary of Education. https://quotefancy.com/quote/1745785/Margaret-Spellings

2. Monroe Levin Memo 6/15/1984.

3. Ibid.

4. Board Minutes 6/2/1984.

5. Committee members: Betty Allen and Jane Ballard (Co-Chairs), Ron Banyay, Grant Beglarian, Catherine Bostron, Richard Casper, Barbara Field, Gary Zeller, Lester Glick, Hadassah Markson, Kalman Novak, Allen Sol Schoenbach, John Smith, and Eloise Sutton.

6. Federation of European Music School Associations. www.musicschoolunion.eu/members/germany.

7. The schools representing the US were: New England Conservatory of Music, Boston, MA; Flint Institute of Music, Flint, MI; Levine School of Music, Washington, D.C.; Music Center of the North Shore, Winnetka, IL; Montclair State College Preparatory Division, Montclair, NJ; MERIT Program, Chicago, IL; The Colburn School, Los Angeles, CA; MacPhail Center for the Arts, Minneapolis, MN.

8. Fundraising Report January 10, 1985.

9. Standards and Evaluation Committee Report, March 2, 1985.

10. Marcy Horwitz memo, June 27, 1980.

Chapter Eleven: Nothing Ventured, Nothing Gained

1. Board Minutes June 5th, 1987.

2. Wolfensohn, a friend of Jacqueline du Pré, began cello studies with her at the age of 41 when she offered to teach him on the condition that he perform on his 50th birthday at Carnegie Hall in New York City, which he did. He repeated the exercise on his 60th and 70th birthdays with Yo-Yo Ma and Bono. He has

appeared, together with musician friends, at private events at Carnegie Hall and elsewhere. [Wikipedia 8/26/2019]

3. Executive Committee Conference Call, December 16, 1987.

Chapter Twelve: Process and Product

No notes

Chapter Thirteen: Field of Dreams

1 *Field of Dreams* – from the 1989 movie of the same name. "Build it and they will come."

2 Jessica Chao remarks, Annual Meeting of the Corporation, National Guild of Community Schools of the Arts, 11/16/91 St. Louis.

3 3/9/90 Letter of invitation to grant-makers from Lolita Mayadas.

4 Correspondence between John Zinsser, Jane Ballard and Lolita Mayadas.

5 Jessica Chao email to Lolita Mayadas 10/3/19.

6 Board Minutes 6/22/91.

7 Lila Wallace–Reader's Digest Fund Press Release 6/25/92. An accompanying memo spelled out the components of the GuildTech Program together with grant amounts: Management Assistance Program (MAP), to include:

- The Arts Management in Community Institutions (AMICI) Program – $25,000 for scholarship and faculty support for one seminar each year.

- The Intensive Seminars Program – $32,150 for scholarship and faculty support for three seminars each year.

- New Arts Schools and Centers (NASCENT) Program – $25,900 to seed four new schools per year for two years.

- Adopt-a-School Model Partnership Program – $60,000 to fund partnerships10 established Guild schools "adopt" 10 smaller schools each year.

- Additional support per year was approved as follows:
    - Panel Review $6,875
    - Two new staff persons $45,000
    - Computer equipment $9,000
    - Rent for extra office space $3,000
    - General support for the Guild $15,050 (for 1992)

8   Richard Evans email dated 10/16/19.

9   A study of members of the National Guild of Community Schools of the Arts : by Richard Evans and Howard Klein; with Jane Delgado. Front Cover. Richard Evans. Lila Wallace–Reader's Digest Fund, 1992 – Artists and community – 86 pages. A Study of the Members of the National Guild of Community Schools of the Arts. Abstract: The report is based on a detailed survey of 93 community schools from which statistical data relating to the schools' programs, management and finances over the last five years were derived and analyzed.

10 Tribute to Lolita Mayadas at the Annual Meeting for 10 years of service. St. Louis 1991.

11 An article in the Arts Section of *The New York Times* recognizes the important role played by the Fund. It is headlined: Wallace Fund Quietly Grows Into Nation's Top Arts Donor, April 2, 1992, Section C, Page 15

12 Ibid.

13 Ibid.

14 Lila Wallace–Reader's Digest Fund Press Release 6/25/91.

- The Cleveland Music School Settlement, Cleveland, Ohio ($400,000)

- Community Music Center, San Francisco, California ($250,000)

- Community School of Music and Arts, Mountain View, California ($180,000)

- David Hochstein Memorial Music School, Rochester, New York ($262,870)

- Hoff-Barthelson Music School, Scarsdale, New York ($300,000)

- The Merit Music Program, Chicago, Illinois ($150,000)

- Settlement Music School, Philadelphia, Pennsylvania ($750,000)

- Third Street Music School Settlement, New York ($577,500)

- Westchester Conservatory of Music, White Plains, New York ($300,000)

15 Wallace Funds: new name for the Lila Wallace–Reader's Digest Funds

Chapter Fourteen: Sea Change

1. Robert Browning, from Cleon.

2. Executive Committee Minutes 11/12/92.

3. Jessica Chao Invitation dated June 1992.

4. Long Range Plan October 1992.

5. Executive Committee Minutes 11/12/92.

6. Board Minutes 11/12/95.

7. Guildnotes Commentaries Sept/Oct 1997 – Cyber Frontiers.

8. Development Report 11/11/94.

   Unrestricted Funds

   - Mary Flagler Cary Trust $12,000

- Horace W. Goldsmith Foundation $12,500

- Seth Sprague Educational and Charitable Foundation $5,000

- Samuel and Rebecca Kardon Foundation $1,000

- NCR Corporation $1,000

Restricted Funds

- Lila Wallace–Reader's Digest Fund $659,000 (3-year grant for GuildTech II)

- Lila Wallace–Reader's Digest Fund: GuildTech $188,000 (3rd year of GuildTech I)

- Vira I. Heinz Endowment $58,000 (Regional GuildTech II)

- William Randolph Hearst Foundation $35,000 (General Endowment)

- Bay and Paul Foundations $32,000 (3rd year of Repro)

- Theodore Presser Foundation $30,000 (NASCENT)

- Foundations of the Milken Families $1,000 (Young Composers Awards)

- John Ben Snow Memorial Trust $7,850 (Artstream Teacher Training)

- Hyde and Watson Foundation $5,000 (Computer Equipment)

Chapter Fifteen: Darkness at Noon

1   Darkness at Noon (German: *Sonnenfinsternis*) is a novel by Hungarian-born British novelist Arthur Koestler, first published in 1940. His best-known work, it is the tale of Rubashov, an Old Bolshevik who is arrested, imprisoned, and tried for treason against the government that he had helped to create.

2   Development and Fundraising Issues.

3   Bob Capanna Memo to Janet Hunt and David Lapin, 1/17/1998.

4   Board Minutes 3/7/1998.

5   Mayadas notes dated 3/10/1997 ref. call to Art Judson.

6   Contemporaneous Letter to Dick Casper from Lolita Mayadas 6/23/1998.

7   Board Minutes 3/7/98 1998-2000 funders.

8   Board Minutes 6/6/1998.

9   Toby Mayman letter to Bob Capanna 2/11/1998.

10   Notes of phone conversation between Lolita Mayadas and Donna Merris 2/5/1998.

Chapter Sixteen: Aftermath

1. Lewis Carroll, *Alice in Wonderland.*

Chapter Seventeen: Creative Communities

1   Compilation of items from Board and Annual Reports 1998-2000.

2   Matching Funds Received for Creative Communities 2000-2001 [Staff Handbook].

- The Bay and Paul Foundations.

- Arthur M. Blank Family Foundation.

- MetLife Foundation

- Pepsi-Cola/Hip-Hop Summit Partnership

- Sony Music Entertainment

3   May 3 attendees. **Scott Shanklin-Peterson**, Senior Deputy Chairman; **Karen Christenson**, Deputy Chair (Grants); **Lee Kessler**, Director of Partnerships; **Doug Herbert,** Director, Education and Access; **Michael McLaughlin**, Director, Millennium Projects and Leadership Initiatives; **Wayne Brown**, Director, Music Program.

4 **Planning Committee: Gloria Cousar**, Assistant Deputy Secretary, Office of Public and Indian Housing, HUD; **Priscilla Dreyman**, Executive Director, SPIRAL Arts, Portland Maine; **Mindy Duitz**, Open Society Institute; **Cynthia Jetter**, Board of Directors, Settlement Music School, Philadelphia, Former Director of Resident Affairs, Philadelphia Housing Authority; **Bruce Jones**, Director, Consortium for Educational Policy Analysis, University of Missouri; **Jonathan Katz** CEO, National Assembly of State Arts Agencies; **Lee Kessler**, Director of Federal Partnerships, NEA; **Donnie LeBoeuf**, Senior Program Manager, Office of Juvenile Justice and Delinquency Prevention, US Department of Justice; **Michael McLaughlin**, Director, Millennium Projects and Leadership Initiatives, NEA; **Robert McNulty**, President, Partners for Livable Communities; and National Guild staff members **Lolita Mayadas**, Executive Director and **Jonathan Herman**, Associate Director. Jonathan Katz is the facilitator.

5 **Advisory Group: Camille** Akeju, Executive Director, Harlem School of the Arts, New York, NY; **Wendy Fleischer**, Economic Development Consultant; currently monitoring the Rockefeller Foundation's *Jobs Plus* program, a demonstration project to raise the rate of employment in six public housing authority sites across the country; **Grady Hillman**, Community Arts Consultant, Austin, TX; Technical Assistance Provider for *Arts Programs for Young Offenders in Detention and Corrections*, a collaborative initiative of the Office of Juvenile Justice Delinquency Prevention and the National Endowment for the Arts; **Latetia Ramirez**, Aide, Jacob Riis Community Center New York, NY, Former President of Tenant's Council; **Joann Williams**, Director, Southeast Branch, Levine School of Music, Washington, DC.

6 Creative Communities Partnership Sites

- Artists Collective, Inc., Hartford, Connecticut

- Center of Contemporary Arts, St. Louis, Missouri

- Children's Art Carnival, New York, New York

- City Arts Center, Oklahoma City, Oklahoma
- Cleveland Public Theatre, Cleveland, Ohio
- Concord Community Music School, Concord, New Hampshire
- Creative Spark, Inc., Mount Pleasant, South Carolina
- Dance Institute of Washington, Washington, District of Columbia
- Federated Dorchester Neighborhood Houses, Inc., Dorchester, Massachusetts
- Los Angeles Music and Art School, Los Angeles, California
- Memphis Black Arts Alliance, Inc., Memphis, Tennessee
- MERIT Music Program, Chicago, Illinois
- Multicultural Education and Counseling through the Arts, Houston, Texas
- Nevada Dance Theatre, Inc., Las Vegas, Nevada
- New Orleans Ballet Association, New Orleans, Louisiana
- Poeh Arts Program/Pueblo of Pojoaque, Santa Fe, New Mexico
- Rhode Island Philharmonic Orchestra, Providence, Rhode Island
- Space One Eleven, Birmingham, Alabama
- Vermont Arts Exchange, North Bennington, Vermont
- Village of Arts and Humanities, Inc., Philadelphia, Pennsylvania

7   CCI Summary Report: Community Schools of the Arts and Public Housing. Findings, Lessons Learned and Successful Strategies for Successful Partnerships. Evaluation 2006

published by the National Guild of Community Schools of the Arts 2006.

Chapter Eighteen: Transitions

1   Members of the Search Committee were: Bob McAllister, Lydia Kontos, Kathy Schumacher, Ellen Breyer, Jonathan Katz, Gayle Morgan, Art Judson II, and Lowell Noteboom, Chair.

2   Memo to the Search Committee from Lowell Noteboom, 10/21/2001.

3   President's Award, now known as the Service Award, is offered for exceptional service to the National Guild and the community arts education movement.

Addendum
Point of View: Lolita Mayadas

From time to time I am asked this question about my tenure at the Guild: "What is your legacy?" I am reminded of Nelson Mandela's answer to that question as conveyed to Morgan Freeman who played the role of Mandela in the movie *Invictus*. When asked, Mandela is said to have responded "No-one will remember."

In my case, if I have any legacy at all, perhaps it lies in the bi-monthly Commentaries I wrote for Guildnotes, which attempt to express what the Guild stood for, what it believed in, what it envisioned, and what will remain, hopefully, long after we have all passed away.

With that in mind, I now append a small selection of the Commentaries.

July/August 2000

In the Mind's Eye

This is an age which has stretched what we know beyond anything we ever knew before. And the more we know, the greater the specialization. And the more the specialization, the less our connection to other fields of learning. We don't hear much any more about knowledge for its own sake or about a "well-rounded" education. Mostly, we speak of skills and expertise. The world we live in seems to demand this level of concentration. But we have paid a price in our Faustian bargain with progress. What we have gained in depth we have lost in breadth. What we have won through single-minded focus we have surely lost in curiosity, or the freedom to roam, or perhaps the imagination.

The mind's eye is not myopic. Set free, it is capable of seeing across the constrictions of specialized thinking, capable of a sort of creative anarchy, capable of putting things together that might seem to have little in common. Perhaps this is what genius is. Though not educated in the formal sense, Beethoven read the classics and the works of the major philosophers. Einstein found something irreplaceable in music. Who can tell what Jefferson's interest in botany did for his ability to draft the Declaration of Independence, or vice-versa? And would Nabokov have been a better writer if he had concentrated more on his craft and less on butterflies? With all of the debates in recent years about the impact of music on learning in other fields we seem to have developed an obsession about cause and effect which may prove to be too narrow and ultimately irrelevant.

January/February 1985

A Question of Merit

Now and again, a catch word becomes popular in the lexicon of certain groups of people. For a while it was "partnerships." Now, the concept of "excellence" seems to be taking hold. Perhaps the ethos of the Second Term has something to do with this. When the word has been squeezed dry by sheer over-usage, it will become a euphemism for something we really don't want to say for fear of upsetting people, like "exceptional" or "special" which used to mean outstanding...

But in its own way, the perception of excellence is already harmful. In everyday usage its meaning is connected with talent or conspicuous ability, not with the less visible efforts to achieve whatever excellence is: the alchemy which opens up a whole range of possibilities through the awakening of latent instincts, creativity, rational thinking, and cognition. It eventually becomes a state of mind, infinitely subtle and unpredictable. Excellence is not as easily recognized as talent. It is, instead, a movable target. Its attainment will always remain maddeningly beyond our grasp since it continues to recede with its own realization. The most celebrated of artists have yet to achieve the excellence they continually seek.

What then is excellence? For some of us who must deal every day with the tussles of teaching those who are not comforted by their inborn gifts, a definition does not come glibly. The best that can be said is that excellence is not the end result but rather, the striving for the end result; it is the continual process through which teacher and pupil move from one plane of achievement to the next. For the talented, the journey may be smoother, but for the rest the effort is particularly laudable for being so very arduous.

<u>June/July 1985</u>

Summer Madness

I hope that my readers will forgive me if I indulge in a little whimsy, resulting possibly from an overdose of reading and researching reams of material for this newsletter. Put it down to the seductions of summer and the partial failure to assimilate all of the information which not only arrives regularly on my desk, but also remains somewhere unseen, just waiting to be discovered. Call it the lament of an overworked administrator, with apologies to Lewis Carroll.

"The time has come," the Turtle said, "to speak of many things."

"What for?" said Alice.

"So that you can listen, of course," said the Mad Hatter. At this point, the Dormouse at the head of the table began to snore.

"Silence," screamed the Red Queen, and turned to Alice, "what have you got to say?"

"Nothing," said Alice a little timidly.

"She's stupid," said the Mad Hatter. "Everyone always has something to say, people are saying things all the time."

"That's silly," said Alice severely. "I don't have to talk to be clever."

The Mad Hatter wet his whiskers in his tea. "No," he said, "but you do have to be clever to talk."

The Turtle cleared this throat and put on his spectacles. "Take notes," he said to Alice.

"I can't," she said, "I haven't anything to write on."

"Never mind," said the Turtle kindly, "use your napkin."

Everyone started to talk at once. "Please," said Alice, "could you speak one at a time?"

"It doesn't matter," said the Caterpillar, "if we all say the same thing. Besides, you only write down what you can hear."

"But I can't hear anything," said Alice, "if everyone talks at the same time."

"All the better," said the Mad Hatter, "then you don't have to write down anything at all."

Suddenly, everyone started to throw their napkins at Alice, who gave a little cry and woke up in her schoolroom where she had gone to sleep on the Sunday *Times*.

July/August 2001

Diversity and Division

What is meant by diversity? It could be defined as the condition of being different or having differences. But in current parlance, diversity most often means being culturally and/or racially different. And we've gotten used to the language of politicians and others who continually affirm and celebrate these so-called differences. But is there a point at which too much diversity could mean too much division? Is there a point at which "community" in America means a collection of communities, each separate and distinct from the other? Is there a point where such self-inflicted segregation becomes the norm? If so, whatever's happening to the American dream of assimilation? According to a Harvard University study, U.S. schools grew more segregated in the 1990's, with schools in New York being the third-most-segregated in the nation. And a newspaper article some months ago spoke of the increasing Balkanization of the city. If you live in Queens, for instance, you are most likely to be from India. There you can live like an Indian; you can preserve and protect your culture, your art, your religion, your schools, your language, and your traditions. You don't really care what they do in Chinatown. You've insulated yourself from all those "alien" cultures. One could call this degree of separation diversity, but is that what we would want it to mean?

Nothing Ventured

Once upon a time, there lived in the green woods of New Hampshire a couple of old codgers who decided to answer the call of the moose during the hunting season. "Well, Jake," said one, "I guess we'd better look for some guy who'd take us out there." The other reflected for a minute. "Yeah, sure," he said. So they dusted off their Bell yellow pages and came up with a man who was both willing and able. The day of departure dawned and everyone set off. As they landed in moose country, the pilot turned to his companions and said, "Now remember, this is a mighty small plane. All it'll take is you 'n me and one small moose – no more'n that, just one small moose."

And with that, he left the two old folks on the ground, promising to be back in three days. On the third day when he returned, he was much annoyed to find his passengers waiting on the landing strip with two large moose, antlers and all. "What did I tell you?" he said. "I ain't taking no more'n one." The two friends went into a huddle. "That's no good," they said. "Last year they took us both _and_ two moose." The pilot scratched his head, thinking of his competition. "O.K.," he said eventually, and packed the two old timers into the plane, then one moose, then the other, and squeezed into his seat.

The plane groaned along the runway and just heaved over the tops of the trees. It tottered along until it met a pine tree, chopped off the top, and crashed into the ground, bits of windows and antlers all over the place. When the dust had settled, one fellow lifted his head out of the wreckage and looked around. "Where'd you think we be, Jake?" he said. "I dunno," said his friend, "but I reckon we're a mile further'n we were last year."

Chalk one up for progress. Anyone who is not amoosed may address complaints directly to the President of the Guild.

<u>January/February 1996</u>

Innovation Recycled

No doubt about it - we Americans live in a throwaway society. When something isn't working, we trash it and get another. Never mind whether it's an appliance, an idea, or a method. Rather than fix it, we prefer to toss it out. We have such a love affair with new and innovative things that we're either unable or unwilling to repair what we have. State-of-the-art is where we're at and where we're going to stay. It isn't such a stretch to apply that mindset to the state of education. How many good ideas of methods have we discarded into the landfills of history? What could we learn from their recycling?

There must be so much that actually worked and that achieved their objectives. In spite of all the cutting-edge responses we like to think up, little of it is really new. Reading through the mounds of literature that are the latest and best on the subject, one can't get away from the suspicion that someone, somewhere, must have done this before. And if so, there's some result we need to know about and learn from. It could be highly instructive to research those archives of disposable experience and reinstate the best of what we've abandoned. Now <u>that</u> could be something really innovative.

<u>September/October 1993</u>

Chicken and Egg

Efforts to preach to the unconverted about the value of the arts are, by and large, focused on their function as catalysts of one kind or another. Rarely is a convincing case made that the arts are important in and of themselves, as are the sciences and humanities. But given chronic budget problems, it is perhaps naive to think that the battle will be won on such purist grounds. As a result, several cause-related strategies seem to be emerging: if only we could convince people that the arts enhance self-esteem, help test scores, improve reading and math skills, build ethnic pride and encourage social interaction, then our job will be done. But that approach could defeat the purpose. Where is the proof that these things are achieved through the arts exclusively?

It may indeed be true that music helps math comprehension. But the converse could also be true: math helps musical comprehension. And if a dance class is good for self-discipline, so is baseball. In reality, these arguments could be used either for, or against, the arts. They obscure the real issues. The arts are important because they are irreplaceable in the education matrix, because they offer unique ways of thinking, feeling, and knowing and because they are indispensable in any society that calls itself civilized. Not presenting the case in this way, with as much supporting evidence as possible, is to run the risk of pushing the arts out even further to the fringes.

<u>January/February 2001</u>

Beauty and the Beast

Rather than write an original commentary, I defer to a provocative piece written by Edward Rothstein in *The New York Times* in February 1998: "Great technology," David Gelernter argues in his book: *Machine Beauty: Elegance and the Heart of Technology*, "is beautiful technology." And the tragedy for a computer scientist like Mr. Gelernter is how ugly computer technology has become. "Commercial software manufacturers," Mr. Gelernter argues, "sell half-finished products, awaiting reports of system crashes and bugs the way potentates used to watch their dinnertime beta testers for signs of poisoning. New software is piled high with irrelevancies and distractions like children's collages of 'gaily painted macaroni' smelling of Elmer's Glue. How," he asks, "did ugliness manage to dominate the game for so long? How could such a beautiful machine like Apple's Macintosh, for example, ever have taken second place to the cloddish design of MS-DOS? And now that Microsoft has adopted Apple's design in Windows, why is it, in its marred form, finally acceptable?"

These are not minor matters. Mr. Gelernter considers beauty to be an essential part of the computer revolution; it is, ideally "a happy marriage of simplicity and power. Right now," he said, "both simplicity and power are sadly lacking." For Mr. Gelernter, who teaches at Yale University, developing new computer technologies, and is the art critic for the *Weekly Standard* magazine, the failure is partly cultural. He believes that art education should be required for software designers (and everyone else). And he attributes the success of PC ugliness to "an American discomfort with elegance."

March/April 1991

Eminent Amateurs

I wonder why and when the word "amateur" was devalued? Everyone knows its Latin roots, but usage has tarnished its original meaning. Sadly, there is no other word that can replace it. How do we define a person who truly loves the arts for their own sake, who will pursue learning for its own sake, who will tinker around worlds beyond his calling? The concept of the amateur has all but disappeared from our thinking. Yet it is at the heart of all education. For a man to be truly educated, he must have knowledge of things far beyond his own profession. Einstein and Schweitzer were musical amateurs. Churchill spent his weekends painting. The curiosity of Thomas Jefferson was that of an inspired amateur, a Renaissance man.

Have we forgotten that we are all amateurs in one sense or another? When we went to school, we were not expected to become professionals in all of our fields of learning. Yet, in the arts we persist in the *canard* that training, real training, is reserved only for those on the way to a career. There are schools for the pre-professional, the incipient professional, the aspiring professional. Where are the schools for the inspired amateurs, the artistic tinkerers, the great, silent majority out there? Without them, the artist is redundant. Let us grasp the problem by its roots. It is in the community schools where the training, real training, of the amateur takes place. In all of our deliberations about artistic quality and mission, I hope we will never forget that.

Bibliography

Addams, Jane. *A Centennial Reader*. New York: The MacMillan Company, 1960.

Creative Communities Initiative Summary Report. New York: National Guild for Community Arts Education, 2006.

Cummins, Paul F. *Dachau Song: The Twentieth Century Odyssey of Herbert Zipper*. New York: Peter Lang, 1992.

Egan, Robert F. *Music and the Arts in the Community: The Community Music School in America*. Metuchen, N.J. & London: Scarecrow Press, 1989.

Evans, Richard, Howard Klein, and Jane C. Delgado. *Too Intrinsic for Renown: a Study of the Members of the National Guild of Community Schools of the Arts, Executive Summary*. New York: Lila Wallace-Reader's Digest Fund, 1991.

Guttman, Jacqueline S. *Partners in Excellence: A Guide to Community School of the Arts/Public School Partnerships – From Inspiration to Implementation*. New York: National Guild of Community Schools of the Arts, 2005.

Mahlman, John J. *Coming to Our Senses: A Panel Report*. The Arts, Education, and Americans Panel, David Rockefeller, Jr., Chairman. New York: McGraw-Hill, 1977.

Mayadas, Azim L. *A Retrospective*. Englewood, N.J.: National Guild of Community Schools of the Arts, 1995.

Schenck, Janet D. *Music Youth and Opportunity: A Survey of Settlement and Community Music Schools.* Boston: National Federation of Settlements, Boston. 1926.

CPSIA information can be obtained
at www.ICGtesting.com
Printed in the USA
BVHW091047180421
605248BV00017B/1391